Southern Living

Celebration Cakes

Recipes
Included!

A LIFESTYLE COLORING BOOK

Illustrated by Jan Gerardi

Oxmoor
House

©2016 Time Inc. Books

Published by Oxmoor House, an imprint of Time Inc. Books
225 Liberty Street, New York, NY 10281

Illustrator: Jan Gerardi
Art Director: Georgia Morrissey
Senior Editor: Katherine Cobbs
Project Editor: Lacie Pinyan
Junior Designer: AnnaMaria Jacob
Associate Project Manager: Hillary Leary
Copy Editor: Donna Baldone
Proofreader: Rebecca Brennan
Fellows: Helena Joseph, Kyle Grace Mills

ISBN-13: 978-0-8487-5220-0
ISBN-10: 0-8487-5220-1

First Edition 2016

Printed in the United States of America

10 9 8 7 6 5 4 3 2 1

Time Inc. Books products may be purchased for business or promotional use. For information on bulk purchases, please contact Christi Crowley in the Special Sales Department at (845) 895-9858.

We welcome your comments and suggestions about Time Inc. Books.
Please write to us at:
Time Inc. Books
Attention: Book Editors
P.O. Box 62310
Tampa, Florida 33662-2310

❧ Welcome! ❧

Channel your inner pastry chef as you render these decadent cakes in a rainbow of color. With more than 60 recipes from the South's most trusted test kitchen at *Southern Living* magazine, this coloring book provides multiple options for from-scratch creations—one-of-a-kind works of art with accompanying recipes on the back of each cake for keeping or giving that can be personalized in your own signature style.

Perfect for all ages and even better when shared, the *Southern Living Celebration Cakes* coloring book lets you bring the party to life with crayons, markers, colored pencils, or pastels. Recipes include Southern classics such as Lane Cake, Red Velvet Cake, and Hummingbird Bundt Cake as well as retro delights such as Ambrosia Cake and Carrot Cake, and so many more. Consider it our sweet gift to you and a perfect gift for others. Enjoy!

Lemon Cheese Layer Cake

Lemon Cheese Layer Cake

Serves 12 to 16 · Hands-on 1 hour 30 minutes · Total 22 hours 45 minutes

Lemon Curd:
- 1¾ cups granulated sugar
- 6 ounces (¾ cup) butter, softened
- 4 large eggs
- 3 large egg yolks
- 1 tablespoon lemon zest
- ¾ cup fresh lemon juice

Cake:
- Shortening
- 1¾ cups granulated sugar
- 8 ounces (1 cup) butter, softened
- 4 large eggs, separated, at room temperature

- 1 tablespoon orange zest
- 3 cups (11.3 ounces) cake flour
- 2½ teaspoons baking powder
- ¼ teaspoon table salt
- 1 cup fresh orange juice
- 3 (4-inch) wooden skewers

Lemon-Orange Buttercream Frosting:
- 3 cups powdered sugar, sifted
- 4 ounces (½ cup) butter, softened
- 1 tablespoon orange zest

1. **Make the Curd:** Beat the first 2 ingredients at medium speed with an electric mixer until blended. Add the 4 eggs and 3 egg yolks, 1 at a time, to the butter mixture, beating just until blended after each addition. Stir in the lemon zest. Gradually add the lemon juice to the butter mixture, beating at low speed just until blended after each addition. (The mixture will look curdled.) Transfer to a large heavy saucepan.

2. Cook the mixture over medium-low, whisking constantly, 14 to 16 minutes or until it thickens, coats the back of a spoon, and starts to mound slightly when stirred. Transfer the mixture to a bowl.

3. Place heavy-duty plastic wrap directly on the surface of the warm curd (to prevent a film from forming), and cool 1 hour. Chill 8 hours.

4. **Make the Cake:** Grease (with shortening) and flour 4 (8-inch) round shiny cake pans. Preheat the oven to 350°F. Beat 1¾ cups granulated sugar and 1 cup softened butter at medium speed with an electric mixer until fluffy. Add 4 egg yolks, 1 at a time, beating just until blended after each addition. Stir in the orange zest.

5. Sift together the flour and next 2 ingredients; gradually add to butter mixture alternately with 1 cup orange juice, beginning and ending with flour mixture, beating just until blended after each addition.

6. Beat the 4 egg whites at medium-high speed with mixer until stiff peaks form. Fold one-third of egg whites into batter; fold remaining egg whites into batter. Pour the batter into prepared pans (about 1¾ cups batter in each pan).

7. Bake at 350°F for 17 to 20 minutes or until a wooden pick inserted in center comes out clean. Cool in pans on wire racks 10 minutes; remove to wire racks, and cool completely (about 30 minutes).

8. Reserve and refrigerate 1 cup of the Lemon Curd. Spread the remaining Lemon Curd between the cake layers and on top of the cake (about ½ cup per layer). Insert skewers 2 to 3 inches apart into the cake to prevent layers from sliding. Immediately wrap cake tightly in plastic wrap, and chill 12 to 24 hours. (The layers of the cake and the Lemon Curd will set and firm up overnight, ripening the flavor and making the cake more secure and easier to frost.)

9. **Make the Frosting:** Beat 1 cup of the powdered sugar, ½ cup butter, and 1 tablespoon orange zest at low speed with electric mixer until blended. Add ½ cup reserved Lemon Curd alternately with remaining 2 cups powdered sugar, beating until blended after each addition. Increase speed to high, and beat 1 to 2 minutes or until fluffy.

10. Remove skewers from the cake; discard skewers. Spread the frosting on the sides of the cake. Spread remaining ½ cup reserved Lemon Curd over top of cake. (Adding a bit of extra Lemon Curd to the top of the cake creates a luxe decorative finish.)

Red Velvet Cake

Red Velvet Cake

Serves 12 to 16 · Hands-on 1 hour 10 minutes · Total 2 hours 10 minutes

Cake:

Shortening
- 1½ cups granulated sugar
- 8 ounces (1 cup) butter, softened
- ½ cup firmly packed light brown sugar
- 4 large eggs, at room temperature
- 2 tablespoons red liquid food coloring
- 1 tablespoon vanilla extract
- 1 (8-ounce) container sour cream
- ½ cup water
- 2½ cups (10.6 ounces) all-purpose soft-wheat flour (such as White Lily)
- ½ cup unsweetened cocoa
- 1 teaspoon baking soda
- ½ teaspoon table salt

Strawberry Glaze:

- ¾ cup strawberry preserves
- ¼ cup almond liqueur

Strawberry Frosting:

- 6 ounces (¾ cup) butter, softened
- 5 cups powdered sugar, sifted
- 1¾ cups diced fresh strawberries

1. Make the Cake: Preheat the oven to 350°F. Grease (with shortening) and flour 3 (9-inch) round shiny cake pans. Beat the granulated sugar and next 2 ingredients at medium speed with an electric mixer until fluffy. Add the eggs, 1 at a time, beating just until blended after each addition. Add the red food coloring and vanilla, beating at low speed just until blended.

2. Stir together the sour cream and ½ cup water until blended. Sift together the flour and next 3 ingredients; gradually add to butter mixture alternately with sour cream mixture, beginning and ending with flour mixture. Spoon the batter into prepared pans (about 2½ cups batter in each pan).

3. Bake at 350°F for 20 to 24 minutes or until a wooden pick inserted in the center comes out clean. Cool in pans on wire racks 10 minutes; remove from pans to wire racks, and cool completely (about 30 minutes).

4. Make the Glaze: Pulse the strawberry preserves in a food processor until smooth; transfer to a microwave-safe bowl. Microwave the strawberry preserves at HIGH 30 to 45 seconds or until melted; stir in the almond liqueur. Brush ¼ cup of the warm glaze over the top of each cooled cake layer. Reserve remaining ¼ cup glaze.

5. Make the Frosting: Beat ¾ cup softened butter at medium speed 20 seconds or until fluffy. Gradually add 5 cups powdered sugar and ½ cup of the diced strawberries, beating at low speed until creamy. Add ¼ cup of the diced strawberries, 1 tablespoon at a time, beating frosting to desired consistency. Reserve remaining 1 cup diced strawberries.

6. Place 1 cake layer, glazed side up, on a serving platter. Spread one-third of the frosting over the cake layer; sprinkle with ½ cup reserved diced strawberries. Repeat the procedure with the second cake layer. Top with remaining cake layer; spread with remaining frosting. Drizzle remaining ¼ cup strawberry glaze over cake.

Jam Cake

Jam Cake

Serves 12 to 16 · Hands-on 1 hour · Total 2 hours

Cake:

Shortening
- 1½ cups sugar
- 8 ounces (1 cup) butter, softened
- 4 large eggs, at room temperature
- 3 cups (12.8 ounces) all-purpose flour
- 2 tablespoons unsweetened cocoa
- 2 teaspoons pumpkin pie spice
- 1 cup buttermilk
- 1 teaspoon baking soda
- 1½ cups seedless blackberry jam
- 1 tablespoon vanilla extract
- 1½ cups finely chopped toasted pecans
- 1 cup peeled and grated Granny Smith apple (about 1 large)

Caramel-Cream Cheese Frosting:

- 2 (8-ounce) packages cream cheese, softened
- 2 ounces (¼ cup) butter, softened
- 2 (13.4-ounce) cans dulce de leche
- 2 to 4 tablespoons whipping cream

1. Make the Cake: Preheat the oven to 350°F. Grease (with shortening) and flour 4 (9-inch) round shiny cake pans. Beat the sugar and 1 cup butter at medium speed with an electric mixer until light and fluffy. Add the eggs, 1 at a time, beating just until blended after each addition.

2. Stir together the flour and next 2 ingredients. Stir together the buttermilk and baking soda in a 2-cup glass measuring cup. Add the flour mixture to butter mixture alternately with buttermilk mixture, beginning and ending with flour mixture. Beat at low speed just until blended after each addition.

3. Stir the jam until smooth. Add the jam and vanilla to butter mixture, and beat at low speed just until blended. Stir in the toasted pecans and grated apple. Spoon the batter into prepared pans (about 2½ cups batter in each pan).

4. Bake at 350°F for 20 to 22 minutes or until a wooden pick inserted in center comes out clean. Cool in pans on wire racks 10 minutes; remove from pans to wire racks, and cool completely (about 30 minutes).

5. Make the Frosting: Beat the cream cheese and ¼ cup softened butter at medium speed with an electric mixer until creamy. Add the dulce de leche, 1 can at a time, beating until blended after each addition. Gradually add 2 tablespoons whipping cream, 1 tablespoon at a time, and beat at medium speed. Add up to 2 tablespoons additional cream, 1 tablespoon at a time, and beat to desired spreading consistency. Spread the frosting between each layer and on the top and the sides of the cake.

Lane Cake

Lane Cake

Serves 12 to 16 · Hands-on 1 hour 30 minutes · Total 15 hours 35 minutes

Cake:
Shortening
2¼ cups sugar
10 ounces (1¼ cups) butter, softened
8 large egg whites, at room temperature
3 cups (12.8 ounces) all-purpose soft-wheat flour (such as White Lily)
4 teaspoons baking powder
1 cup water
1 tablespoon vanilla extract

Peach Filling:
Boiling water
8 ounces dried peach halves

4 ounces (½ cup) butter, melted
1 cup sugar
8 large egg yolks
¾ cup sweetened flaked coconut
¾ cup chopped toasted pecans
½ cup bourbon
2 teaspoons vanilla extract

Peach Schnapps Frosting:
2 large egg whites
1½ cups sugar
½ cup peach schnapps
2 teaspoons light corn syrup
⅛ teaspoon table salt

1. Make the Cake: Preheat the oven to 350°F. Grease (with shortening) and flour 4 (9-inch) round shiny cake pans. Beat the sugar and butter at medium speed with an electric mixer until fluffy. Gradually add the 8 egg whites, 2 at a time, beating well after each addition.

2. Sift together the flour and baking powder; gradually add to the butter mixture alternately with 1 cup water, beginning and ending with the flour mixture. Stir in 1 tablespoon vanilla. Spoon the batter into prepared pans (about 1¾ cups batter in each pan).

3. Bake at 350°F for 14 to 16 minutes or until a wooden pick inserted in the center comes out clean. Cool in pans on wire racks 10 minutes; remove from pans to wire racks, and cool completely (about 30 minutes).

4. Make the Filling: Pour boiling water to cover over dried peach halves in a medium bowl; let stand 30 minutes. Drain well, and cut into ¼-inch pieces. (After plumping and dicing, you should have about 2 cups peaches.)

5. Whisk together the melted butter and next 2 ingredients in a heavy saucepan. Cook over medium-low, whisking constantly, 10 to 12 minutes or until thickened. Remove from the heat, and stir in the diced peaches, coconut, and next 3 ingredients. Cool completely (about 30 minutes).

6. Spread the filling between cake layers (a little over 1 cup per layer). Cover cake with plastic wrap, and chill 12 hours.

7. Make the Frosting: Pour water to a depth of 1½ inches into a small saucepan; bring to a boil over medium. Whisk together the 2 egg whites, 1½ cups sugar, and next 3 ingredients in a heatproof bowl; place the bowl over boiling water. Beat the egg white mixture at medium-high speed with a handheld electric mixer 12 to 15 minutes or until stiff, glossy peaks form and the frosting is spreading consistency. Remove from the heat, and spread immediately over the top and the sides of the cake.

Coconut Chiffon Cake

Coconut Chiffon Cake

Serves 12 to 16 · Hands-on 1 hour 15 minutes · Total 14 hours 25 minutes

Cake:

Shortening

2½ cups (9.4 ounces) sifted cake flour

1⅓ cups granulated sugar

1 tablespoon baking powder

½ teaspoon table salt

½ cup canola oil

5 large eggs, separated, at room temperature

1 tablespoon vanilla extract

¾ cup water

½ teaspoon cream of tartar

Coconut-Mascarpone Filling:

1 (8-ounce) container mascarpone cheese

½ cup powdered sugar

1 tablespoon vanilla extract

¾ cup whipping cream

1 (6-ounce) package frozen grated coconut, thawed

White Chocolate Buttercream Frosting:

1½ (4-ounce) white chocolate baking bars, chopped

2 tablespoons whipping cream

8 ounces (1 cup) butter, softened

3 cups sifted powdered sugar

2 teaspoons vanilla extract

3 cups sweetened flaked coconut

1. Make the Cake: Preheat the oven to 350°F. Grease (with shortening) and flour 4 (8-inch) round shiny cake pans. Stir together the sifted cake flour and next 3 ingredients in the bowl of a heavy-duty electric stand mixer. Make a well in the center of the flour mixture; add the oil, egg yolks, vanilla, and ¾ cup water. Beat at medium speed 1 to 2 minutes or until smooth.

2. Beat the egg whites and cream of tartar at medium-high speed until stiff peaks form. Fold one-third of egg whites into batter; fold remaining whites into the batter. Spoon the batter into prepared pans (about 2 cups batter in each pan).

3. Bake at 350°F for 12 to 14 minutes or until a wooden pick inserted in center comes out clean. (Do not overbake—cakes will be a very pale golden color.) Cool in pans on wire racks 10 minutes; remove from pans to wire racks, and cool completely (about 30 minutes).

4. Make the Filling: Stir together the mascarpone cheese, ½ cup powdered sugar, and 1 tablespoon vanilla in a large bowl just until blended.

5. Beat ¾ cup cream at low speed with an electric mixer until foamy; increase speed to medium-high, and beat until soft peaks form. Fold the whipped cream into the mascarpone mixture until well blended. Add the thawed grated coconut, and stir just until blended. Spread the mixture between the cake layers (about 1⅓ cups per layer). Cover with plastic wrap, and chill 12 hours.

6. Make the White Chocolate Buttercream Frosting: Microwave the chopped white chocolate and 2 tablespoons whipping cream in a microwave-safe bowl at MEDIUM (50% power) 1 to 1½ minutes or until melted and smooth, stirring at 30-second intervals. Cool completely (about 20 minutes).

7. Beat 1 cup softened butter and 2 cups of the powdered sugar at low speed with an electric mixer until blended. Add the white chocolate mixture, 2 teaspoons vanilla, and remaining 1 cup powdered sugar, and beat at high speed 2 to 3 minutes or until fluffy. Spread the frosting on the top and the sides of the cake. Cover the top and the sides of the cake with 3 cups flaked coconut, gently pressing the coconut into the frosting.

Carrot Cake with
Chèvre Frosting

Carrot Cake with Chèvre Frosting

Serves 8 · Hands-on 40 minutes · Total 2 hours 35 minutes

Cake:

Shortening

Parchment paper

- 2 cups (8.5 ounces) all-purpose flour
- 2 teaspoons baking soda
- 1 teaspoon table salt
- 1 teaspoon ground cinnamon
- 2 cups sugar
- 1¼ cups canola oil
- 3 large eggs
- 3 cups grated carrots
- 1 (8-ounce) can crushed pineapple in juice, drained
- 1¼ cups coarsely chopped walnuts, toasted
- 2 tablespoons minced fresh ginger

Vanilla Chèvre Frosting:

- 2 (4-ounce) goat cheese logs
- 4 ounces (½ cup) butter, softened
- 1 (16-ounce) package powdered sugar
- 1 vanilla bean, split lengthwise

Garnishes: walnuts, carrot curls

1. Make the Cake: Preheat the oven to 350°F. Grease (with shortening) 2 (8-inch) round cake pans; line bottoms with parchment paper, and grease (with shortening) and flour paper.

2. Stir together flour and next 3 ingredients.

3. Whisk together sugar and oil in a large bowl until well blended. Add eggs, 1 at a time, whisking until blended after each addition. Add the flour mixture, stirring just until blended. Fold in the carrots and next 3 ingredients. Spoon the batter into prepared cake pans.

4. Bake at 350°F for 40 to 45 minutes or until a wooden pick inserted in center comes out clean. Cool in pans on wire racks 15 minutes. Remove from pans to wire racks; carefully remove parchment paper, and discard. Cool completely (about 1 hour).

5. Make the Frosting: Beat the goat cheese and ½ cup softened butter at medium speed with an electric mixer 2 to 3 minutes or until creamy. Add the powdered sugar, 1 cup at a time, beating at low speed until blended after each addition. Scrape vanilla bean seeds into goat cheese mixture; discard vanilla pod. Beat 30 seconds to 1 minute or until frosting is light and fluffy.

6. Spread ½ cup frosting between cake layers; spread remaining frosting on top and sides of cake.

Italian Cream Cake

Italian Cream Cake

Serves 20 · Hands-on 15 minutes · Total 1 hour 50 minutes

Cake:

Shortening
- 4 ounces (½ cup) butter, softened
- ½ cup shortening
- 2 cups sugar
- 5 large eggs, separated
- 1 tablespoon vanilla extract
- 2 cups (8.5 ounces) all-purpose flour
- 1 teaspoon baking soda
- 1 cup buttermilk
- 1 cup sweetened flaked coconut

Nutty Cream Cheese Frosting:

- 1 (8-ounce) package cream cheese, softened
- 4 ounces (½ cup) butter, softened
- 1 tablespoon vanilla extract
- 1 (16-ounce) package sifted powdered sugar
- 1 cup toasted chopped pecans

Garnish: toasted pecan halves

1. Make the Cake: Preheat the oven to 350°F. Grease (with shortening) and flour 3 (9-inch) round cake pans. Beat the butter and ½ cup shortening in a large bowl at medium speed with an electric mixer until creamy; gradually add sugar, beating well. Add the egg yolks, 1 at a time, beating until blended after each addition. Add the vanilla; beat just until blended.

2. Combine the flour and baking soda; add to butter mixture alternately with buttermilk, beginning and ending with flour mixture. Beat at low speed just until blended after each addition. Stir in the coconut.

3. Beat the egg whites until stiff peaks form; fold into batter. Pour the batter into prepared pans.

4. Bake at 350°F for 25 minutes or until a wooden pick inserted in center comes out clean. Cool in pans on wire racks 10 minutes. Remove from pans to wire racks, and cool completely (about 1 hour).

5. Make the Frosting: Beat the cream cheese, ½ cup butter, and 1 tablespoon vanilla at medium speed with an electric mixer until creamy. Add the powdered sugar, beating at low speed until blended. Beat the frosting at high speed until smooth; stir in pecans. Spread the Nutty Cream Cheese Frosting between layers and on top and sides of cake.

Caramel Coconut Cream Cake

Caramel Coconut Cream Cake

Serves 12 · Hands-on 55 minutes · Total 2 hours 25 minutes

Cake:

Shortening

4	ounces (½ cup) butter, softened
½	cup shortening
1½	cups granulated sugar
½	cup firmly packed dark brown sugar
5	large eggs, separated
1	tablespoon vanilla extract
2	cups (8.5 ounces) all-purpose flour
1	teaspoon baking soda
1	cup buttermilk
1	cup finely chopped toasted pecans
1	cup sweetened flaked coconut

Quick Caramel Frosting:

8	ounces (1 cup) butter
1	cup firmly packed light brown sugar
1	cup firmly packed dark brown sugar
½	cup heavy cream
4	cups powdered sugar
2	teaspoons vanilla extract

Cream Cheese Frosting:

1	(8-ounce) package cream cheese, softened
4	ounces (½ cup) butter, softened
1	(16-ounce) package powdered sugar
1	teaspoon vanilla extract
3	cups toasted shaved coconut

1. Make the Cake: Preheat the oven to 350°F. Grease (with shortening) 3 (9-inch) round cake pans. Beat the butter and ½ cup shortening at medium speed with an electric mixer until fluffy; gradually add granulated and brown sugars, beating well. Add the egg yolks, 1 at a time, beating until blended after each addition. Add the vanilla, beating until blended.

2. Combine the flour and baking soda; add to butter mixture alternately with buttermilk, beginning and ending with flour mixture. Beat at low speed just until blended after each addition. Stir in the pecans and 1 cup sweetened flaked coconut.

3. Beat the egg whites at high speed until stiff peaks form, and fold into batter. Pour the batter into prepared pans.

4. Bake at 350°F for 23 to 25 minutes or until a wooden pick inserted in center comes out clean.

Cool in pans on wire racks 10 minutes; remove from pans to wire racks, and cool completely (about 1 hour).

5. Make the Quick Caramel Frosting: Bring the butter and sugars to a rolling boil in a 3½-quart saucepan over medium, whisking constantly (about 7 minutes). Stir in the cream, and bring to a boil; remove from heat. Pour into bowl of a heavy-duty electric stand mixer. Gradually beat in the powdered sugar and vanilla at medium speed, using whisk attachment; beat 8 to 12 minutes or until thickened. Immediately spread frosting between layers and on top of cake.

6. Make the Cream Cheese Frosting: Beat the cream cheese and butter at medium speed with an electric mixer until fluffy. Gradually add the powdered sugar, beating at low speed until blended; add vanilla, beating until blended. Spread the Cream Cheese Frosting over sides of cake; press toasted shaved coconut onto sides of cake.

Ambrosia Cake

Ambrosia Cake

Serves 12 · Hands-on 30 minutes · Total 11 hours

Cake:
Shortening
8 ounces (1 cup) butter, softened
2 cups sugar
4 large eggs, separated
3 cups (12.8 ounces) all-purpose flour
1 tablespoon baking powder
½ cup milk
½ cup coconut milk
1 teaspoon vanilla extract
¼ teaspoon coconut extract
⅛ teaspoon table salt

Vanilla Buttercream:
8 ounces (1 cup) butter, softened
2 teaspoons vanilla extract
3¾ cups powdered sugar
¾ to 1 cup heavy cream

Ambrosia Filling:
1 orange
1 (8-ounce) can crushed pineapple, drained
¾ cup sugar
1 tablespoon cornstarch
¼ teaspoon table salt
¾ cup heavy cream
3 large egg yolks
2 tablespoons butter
¼ teaspoon coconut extract
1 cup toasted sweetened flaked coconut

Garnishes: toasted coconut shavings, maraschino cherries, edible flowers, candied orange slices, orange zest curls, fresh pineapple pieces

1. **Make the Cake:** Preheat the oven to 350°F. Grease (with shortening) and flour 3 (9-inch) round cake pans. Beat the butter at medium speed with a heavy-duty electric stand mixer until fluffy; gradually add sugar, beating well. Add the egg yolks, 1 at a time, beating just until blended after each addition.

2. Combine the flour and baking powder; stir together milk and coconut milk. Add the flour mixture to butter mixture alternately with milk mixture, beginning and ending with flour mixture. Beat at low speed until blended after each addition. Stir in the extracts.

3. Beat the egg whites and salt at high speed until stiff peaks form. Stir about one-third egg whites into batter; fold in remaining egg whites. Spoon the batter into prepared pans.

4. Bake at 350°F for 18 to 22 minutes or until a wooden pick inserted in center comes out clean. Cool in pans on wire racks 10 minutes; remove from pans to wire racks, and cool completely (about 1 hour).

5. **Make the Buttercream:** Beat the butter at medium speed with an electric mixer until creamy. Gradually add 1 teaspoon of the vanilla and 1 cup of the powdered sugar. Gradually add remaining 2¾ cups powdered sugar alternately with ¾ cup to 1 cup heavy cream, beating at low speed until blended after each addition. Stir in remaining 1 teaspoon vanilla. Beat at high speed until smooth.

6. Place 1 cake layer on a serving platter. Spoon ⅓ cup of the Vanilla Buttercream into a zip-top plastic bag. Snip 1 corner of bag to make a small hole. Pipe a ring of frosting around cake layer just inside the top edge.

7. **Make the Filling:** Grate zest from orange to equal 2 teaspoons. Peel and section orange; chop segments. Place orange and pineapple in a wire-mesh strainer, and drain. Whisk together the sugar, cornstarch, and salt in a 3-quart saucepan. Whisk in the heavy cream and egg yolks. Bring to a boil over medium, whisking constantly; boil 1 minute or until thickened. Remove from heat; whisk in butter and coconut extract. Stir in orange-pineapple mixture, coconut, and orange zest. Transfer to a bowl, place plastic wrap directly on filling, and chill 8 to 48 hours. Top cake layer with half of the Ambrosia Filling, and spread to edge of ring. Top with a second cake layer. Repeat procedure with ⅓ cup of the frosting and remaining filling. Top with remaining cake layer, and spread remaining frosting on top and sides of cake.

Toasted Almond Butter Cake

Toasted Almond Butter Cake

Serves 12 · Hands-on 25 minutes · Total 2 hours 11 minutes

Cake:

Shortening
- 4 ounces (½ cup) butter, softened
- 2 cups sugar
- 5 large eggs, separated
- 2¼ cups (9.6 ounces) all-purpose flour
- 1¼ teaspoons baking soda
- 1 cup plus 2 tablespoons buttermilk
- 1 teaspoon almond extract
- 1 cup sweetened flaked coconut
- 1½ cups slivered toasted almonds

5-Cup Cream Cheese Frosting:

- 2 (8-ounce) packages cream cheese, softened
- 4 ounces (½ cup) butter, softened
- 2 (16-ounce) packages powdered sugar
- 2 teaspoons vanilla extract

1. Make the Cake: Preheat the oven to 350°F. Grease (with shortening) and flour 3 (9-inch) round cake pans. Beat the butter at medium speed with an electric mixer until creamy. Gradually add the sugar, beating well. Add the egg yolks, 1 at a time, beating until blended after each addition.

2. Combine the flour and baking soda; add to butter mixture alternately with buttermilk, beginning and ending with flour mixture. Beat at low speed just until blended after each addition. Stir in the almond extract and coconut. Chop 1 cup of the almonds; add to batter.

3. Beat the egg whites at high speed until stiff peaks form; fold into batter. Pour batter into prepared pans.

4. Bake at 350°F for 20 to 22 minutes or until a wooden pick inserted in center comes out clean. Cool in pans on wire racks 10 minutes. Remove from pans to wire racks, and cool completely (about 1 hour).

5. Make the Frosting: Beat the cream cheese and butter at medium speed with an electric mixer until creamy. Gradually add the powdered sugar, beating until fluffy. Stir in the vanilla. Spread the 5-Cup Cream Cheese Frosting between layers and on top and sides of cake. Sprinkle with remaining ½ cup slivered almonds.

Luscious Lemon Cake

Luscious Lemon Cake

Serves 12 · Hands-on 20 minutes · Total 1 hour 52 minutes

Cake:
Shortening
8 large egg yolks
6 ounces (¾ cup) butter, softened
1¼ cups sugar
2½ cups (9.4 ounces) cake flour
1 tablespoon baking powder
¼ teaspoon table salt
¾ cup milk
1 teaspoon lemon zest
1 teaspoon fresh lemon juice
1 teaspoon vanilla extract

Luscious Lemon Frosting:
8 ounces (1 cup) butter, softened
2 teaspoons lemon zest
¼ cup fresh lemon juice
2 (16-ounce) packages powdered sugar
2 tablespoons half-and-half

1. **Make the Cake:** Preheat the oven to 375°F. Grease (with shortening) and flour 3 (8-inch) cake pans. Beat the egg yolks at high speed with an electric mixer 4 minutes or until thick and pale.

2. Beat the butter at medium speed until creamy; gradually add sugar, beating well. Add the beaten egg yolks, beating well.

3. Combine the flour, baking powder, and salt; add to butter mixture alternately with milk, beginning and ending with flour mixture. Beat at low speed just until blended after each addition. Stir in the lemon zest, lemon juice, and vanilla. Spoon the batter into prepared pans.

4. Bake at 375°F for 12 to 17 minutes or until a wooden pick inserted in center comes out clean. Cool in pans on wire racks 10 minutes. Remove from pans to wire racks, and cool completely (about 1 hour).

5. **Make the Frosting:** Beat the butter at medium speed with an electric mixer until creamy; stir in lemon zest and lemon juice. (Mixture will appear curdled.) Gradually add powdered sugar; beat at high speed 4 minutes or to desired spreading consistency. Gradually beat in up to 2 tablespoons half-and-half, if necessary, for desired consistency. Spread the Luscious Lemon Frosting on top of the cake and between layers. Cover and chill until ready to serve.

Lemon-Coconut Cake

Lemon-Coconut Cake

Serves 12 · Hands-on 30 minutes · Total 50 minutes

Cake:
Shortening
8 ounces (1 cup) butter, softened
2 cups sugar
4 large eggs, separated
3 cups (12.8 ounces) all-purpose flour
1 tablespoon baking powder
1 cup milk
1 teaspoon vanilla extract

Lemon Filling:
1 cup sugar
¼ cup cornstarch
1 cup boiling water
4 large egg yolks, lightly beaten
2 teaspoons lemon zest
⅓ cup fresh lemon juice
2 tablespoons butter

Cream Cheese Frosting:
1 (8-ounce) package cream cheese, softened
4 ounces (½ cup) butter, softened
1 (16-ounce) package powdered sugar
1 teaspoon vanilla extract
2 cups sweetened flaked coconut

1. Make the Cake: Preheat the oven to 350°F. Grease (with shortening) and flour 3 (9-inch) round cake pans. Beat the butter at medium speed with an electric mixer until fluffy; gradually add sugar, beating well. Add the egg yolks, 1 at a time, beating until blended after each addition.

2. Combine the flour and baking powder; add to butter mixture alternately with milk, beginning and ending with flour mixture. Beat at low speed until blended after each addition. Stir in the vanilla.

3. Beat the egg whites at high speed with electric mixer until stiff peaks form; fold one-third of the egg whites into batter. Gently fold in remaining beaten egg whites just until blended. Spoon the batter into prepared pans.

4. Bake at 350°F for 18 to 20 minutes or until a wooden pick inserted in center comes out clean. Cool in pans on wire racks 10 minutes. Remove from pans to wire racks, and cool completely (about 1 hour).

5. Make the Filling: Combine the sugar and cornstarch in a medium saucepan; whisk in boiling water. Cook over medium, whisking constantly, until sugar and cornstarch dissolve (about 2 minutes). Gradually whisk about one-fourth of hot sugar mixture into egg yolks; add to remaining hot sugar mixture in pan, whisking constantly. Whisk in the lemon zest and lemon juice. Cook, whisking constantly, until mixture is thickened (about 2 to 3 minutes). Remove from heat. Whisk in the butter; cool completely, stirring occasionally. Spread the Lemon Filling between layers.

6. Make the Frosting: Beat the cream cheese and butter at medium speed with an electric mixer until fluffy. Gradually add the powdered sugar, beating at low speed until blended; add vanilla, beating until blended. Spread the Cream Cheese Frosting on top and sides of cake. Sprinkle top and sides with coconut.

Strawberry Mousse Cake

Strawberry Mousse Cake

Serves 10 to 12 · Hands-on 45 minutes · Total 5 hours 15 minutes

Cake:
Shortening
10 ounces (1¼ cups) butter, softened
2¼ cups sugar
7 large egg whites, at room temperature
3½ cups (13.1 ounces) cake flour
4 teaspoons baking powder
1 cup water
2 teaspoons vanilla extract
½ teaspoon almond extract

Strawberry Mousse:
1 envelope unflavored gelatin
¼ cup water
2 cups sliced fresh strawberries
¼ cup sugar
1 cup whipping cream

Fresh Strawberry Frosting:
6 ounces (¾ cup) butter, softened
5 cups powdered sugar
¾ cup finely chopped fresh strawberries

Garnishes: halved fresh strawberries, edible flowers

1. Make the Cake: Preheat the oven to 350°F. Grease (with shortening) and flour 4 (8-inch) round cake pans. Beat the butter and sugar at medium speed with a heavy-duty electric stand mixer until fluffy. Gradually add the egg whites, one-third at a time, beating well after each addition.

2. Sift together the cake flour and baking powder; gradually add to butter mixture alternately with 1 cup water, beginning and ending with flour mixture. Stir in the vanilla and almond extracts. Pour the batter into prepared pans.

3. Bake at 350°F for 22 to 25 minutes or until a wooden pick inserted in center comes out clean. Cool in pans on wire racks 10 minutes. Remove from pans to wire racks, and cool completely (about 30 minutes).

4. Make the Mousse: Sprinkle gelatin over ¼ cup water in a small bowl; let stand 5 minutes. Process the strawberries and sugar in a blender or food processor until smooth, stopping to scrape down sides as needed. Transfer the strawberry mixture to a small saucepan; bring to a boil over medium-high. Remove from heat. Add the gelatin to strawberry mixture, stirring constantly until gelatin dissolves. Cover and chill until consistency of unbeaten egg whites, stirring occasionally (about 30 minutes). Beat the whipping cream at low speed until foamy; increase speed to medium-high, and beat until soft peaks form. Fold the whipped cream into strawberry mixture until well blended. Cover and chill 30 minutes or just until mixture is thick enough to hold its shape when mounded. Spread about 1 cup of the Strawberry Mousse between each cake layer, leaving a ¼-inch border around edges; cover and chill 3 hours or until mousse is set.

5. Make the Frosting: Beat the butter at medium speed 20 seconds or until fluffy. Gradually add the powdered sugar and ¾ cup finely chopped fresh strawberries, beating at low speed until creamy. Spread the Fresh Strawberry Frosting on top and sides of cake.

Strawberries-and-Cream Cake

Strawberries-and-Cream Cake

Serves 12 · Hands-on 30 minutes · Total 10 hours 22 minutes

Cake:

Shortening
- 2 cups (7.5 ounces) sifted cake flour
- 2½ teaspoons baking powder
- ½ teaspoon table salt
- 1¼ cups sugar
- ½ cup canola oil
- ¼ cup fresh lemon juice
- 4 large egg yolks
- ¼ cup water
- 8 large egg whites
- 1 teaspoon cream of tartar

Strawberry Jam Filling:

- 4 cups mashed fresh strawberries
- 2½ cups sugar
- 1 (3-ounce) package strawberry-flavored gelatin

Strawberries-and-Cream Frosting:

- 1 tablespoon strawberry-flavored gelatin
- 2 tablespoons boiling water
- 1 cup whipping cream
- ¼ cup sugar
- 1 (8-ounce) container sour cream

Garnishes: fresh mint leaves, edible flowers

1. Make the Cake: Preheat the oven to 350°F. Grease (with shortening) and flour 6 (8-inch) round cake pans. Stir together cake flour, baking powder, salt, and 1 cup of the sugar in a large bowl. Make a well in center of mixture; add oil, next 2 ingredients, and ¼ cup water. Beat at medium-high speed with an electric mixer 3 to 4 minutes or until smooth.

2. Beat the egg whites and cream of tartar at medium-high speed until soft peaks form. Gradually add remaining ¼ cup sugar, 1 tablespoon at a time, beating until stiff peaks form. Gently stir one-fourth of egg white mixture into flour mixture; gently fold in remaining egg white mixture. Spoon the batter into prepared pans.

3. Bake at 350°F for 12 to 15 minutes or until a wooden pick inserted in center comes out clean. Cool in pans on wire racks 10 minutes; remove from pans to wire racks, and cool completely (about 1 hour).

4. Make the Filling: Stir together the mashed fresh strawberries and sugar in a large saucepan; let stand 30 minutes. Bring the strawberry mixture to a boil over medium; boil 5 minutes. Remove from heat, and stir in gelatin until dissolved; cool completely (about 1 hour). Cover and chill 8 hours. Spread the Strawberry Jam Filling between cake layers, leaving a ¼-inch border around edges (about ⅔ cup between each layer). Cover the cake with plastic wrap, and chill 8 to 24 hours.

5. Make the Frosting: Stir together the strawberry-flavored gelatin and 2 tablespoons boiling water in a small bowl; cool completely (about 20 minutes). Beat the whipping cream and gelatin mixture at high speed with an electric mixer until foamy; gradually add sugar, beating until soft peaks form. Stir in the sour cream, ¼ cup at a time, stirring just until blended after each addition. Spread the Strawberries-and-Cream Frosting on top and sides of cake. Chill 2 hours before serving.

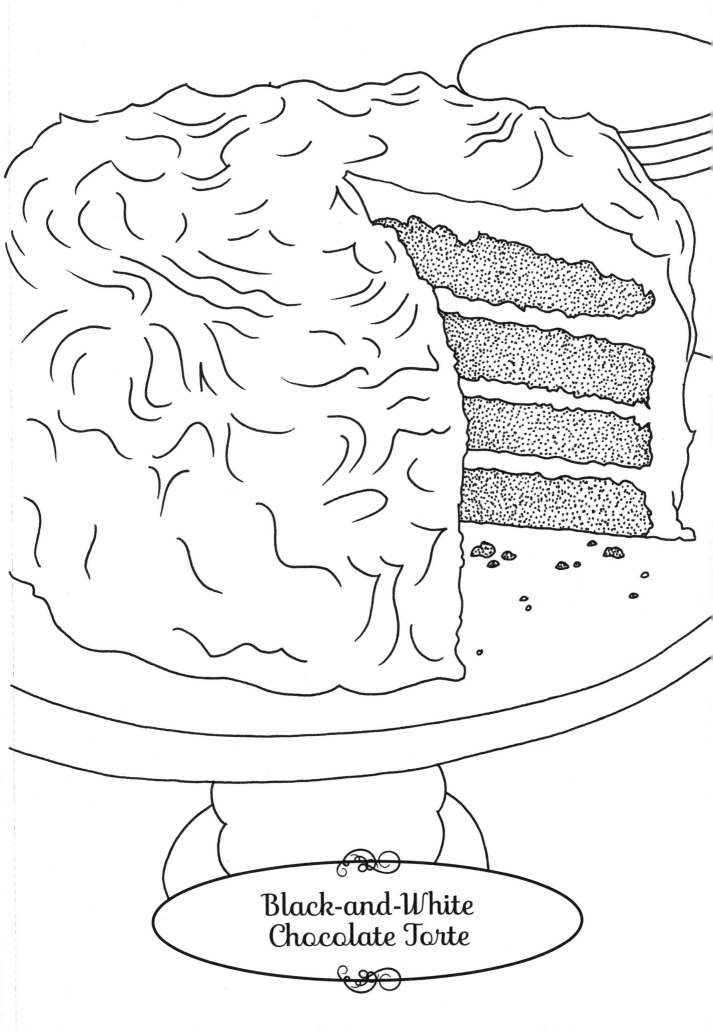

Black-and-White
Chocolate Torte

Black-and-White Chocolate Torte

Serves 12 · Hands-on 45 minutes · Total 2 hours 45 minutes

Cake:
Shortening
3   (1-ounce) unsweetened chocolate baking squares, chopped
4   ounces (½ cup) butter
1   cup hot water
2   cups (8.5 ounces) all-purpose flour
2   cups firmly packed brown sugar
1½   teaspoons baking soda
½   teaspoon table salt
2   large eggs

½   cup sour cream
1   teaspoon vanilla extract
⅓   cup granulated sugar
⅓   cup coffee-flavored liqueur
1   tablespoon water

White Chocolate Whipped Cream:
½   cup whipping cream
12   ounces white chocolate baking bars
3   cups whipping cream

1. Make the Cake: Preheat the oven to 350°F. Grease (with shortening) and lightly flour bottoms only of 2 (8- or 9-inch) round cake pans.

2. Cook chocolate, butter, and 1 cup hot water in a 2-quart saucepan over medium, stirring occasionally, until melted and smooth. Remove from heat; cool 5 minutes. Stir together the flour, brown sugar, baking soda, and salt in a large bowl. Add the melted chocolate mixture, beating at medium speed with an electric mixer just until blended. Add the eggs, 1 at a time, beating until blended. Beat in the sour cream and vanilla. Pour the batter into prepared pans.

3. Bake at 350°F for 30 to 32 minutes or until a wooden pick inserted in center comes out clean. Cool in pans on wire racks 10 minutes. Remove from pans to wire racks, and cool completely (about 1 hour).

4. Meanwhile, stir together the granulated sugar, liqueur, and 1 tablespoon water in a 1-quart saucepan. Bring to a boil over medium, stirring occasionally, until sugar is dissolved; remove from heat. Cool completely.

5. Make the White Chocolate Whipped Cream: Microwave the whipping cream and white chocolate in a microwave-safe glass bowl at HIGH 45 to 60 seconds or until chocolate is melted and smooth, stirring at 30-second intervals. Cover surface directly with plastic wrap (to prevent a film from forming); refrigerate 30 minutes or until cooled but not firm. Beat the white chocolate mixture and whipping cream in a large bowl at medium speed with an electric mixer until soft peaks form.

6. Using a serrated knife, slice the cake layers in half horizontally to make 4 layers. Brush about 2 tablespoons of the liqueur mixture over cut side of each layer; let stand 1 minute.

7. Place 1 cake layer, cut side up, on serving plate; spread with 1 cup of the White Chocolate Whipped Cream to within ¼ inch of edge. Top with another layer, cut side down; spread with 1 cup of the whipped cream mixture. Repeat with remaining layers. Spread top and sides of cake with remaining whipped cream mixture. Store loosely covered in refrigerator.

Chocolate Turtle Cake

Chocolate Turtle Cake

Serves 16 · Hands-on 40 minutes · Total 4 hours 25 minutes

Shortening
Unsweetened cocoa
1 (15.25-ounce) package devil's food cake mix
1 (3.9-ounce) package chocolate instant pudding mix
3 large eggs
1¼ cups milk
1 cup canola oil
1 tablespoon vanilla extract
1 teaspoon instant coffee granules

1 (6-ounce) package semisweet chocolate morsels
1 cup chopped pecans
1 (16-ounce) container ready-to-spread cream cheese frosting
½ cup canned dulce de leche
2 (7-ounce) packages turtle candies
1 (12-ounce) jar caramel ice-cream topping
¼ cup toasted pecan halves

1. Preheat the oven to 350°F. Grease (with shortening) 2 (9-inch) round cake pans; dust with cocoa.

2. Beat the cake mix and next 6 ingredients at low speed with an electric mixer for 1 minute. Beat at medium speed 2 minutes. Fold in the chocolate morsels and chopped pecans. Pour the batter into prepared pans.

3. Bake at 350°F for 30 to 32 minutes or until a wooden pick inserted in center comes out clean. Cool in pans on wire racks 10 minutes. Remove from pans to wire racks, and cool completely (about 1 hour). Wrap cake layers in plastic wrap; refrigerate at least 1 hour.

4. Whisk together frosting and dulce de leche in a medium bowl until well blended. Cut 6 of the turtle candies in half; set aside for garnish. Chop remaining candies.

5. Place 1 cake layer, top side up, on serving plate. Spread with half of the frosting mixture; sprinkle with chopped candies. Place second cake layer, top side up, on candies. Spread remaining frosting mixture on top of cake. Cover; refrigerate until serving time. Drizzle the caramel topping over top of cake, allowing some to drip down sides. Top the cake with pecan halves and reserved turtle candies.

Chocolate Peppermint
Layer Cake

Chocolate Peppermint Layer Cake

Serves 12 to 16 · Hands-on 30 minutes · Total 2 hours 10 minutes

Cake:

Shortening

Parchment paper

2 cups granulated sugar

2 cups (9 ounces) all-purpose flour

1 teaspoon baking soda

½ teaspoon table salt

8 ounces (1 cup) unsalted butter

¼ cup unsweetened dark cocoa

1 cup water

3 ounces bittersweet chocolate, chopped

½ cup buttermilk

2 large eggs, lightly beaten

1 teaspoon vanilla extract

Peppermint Buttercream Frosting:

12 ounces (1½ cups) unsalted butter, softened

8 cups powdered sugar, sifted

1 teaspoon vanilla extract

½ teaspoon peppermint extract

⅛ teaspoon table salt

¼ cup heavy cream

½ cup crushed peppermint stick candies

2 drops of red liquid food coloring

White Chocolate Snowflakes:

Parchment paper

4 ounces white chocolate, chopped

Garnishes: white chocolate curls,
White Chocolate Snowflakes

1. Make the Cake: Preheat the oven to 350°F. Grease (with shortening) 2 (8-inch) round cake pans. Line pans with parchment paper; grease parchment paper, and dust with flour.

2. Combine the granulated sugar, flour, baking soda, and salt in a large bowl. Bring the butter, cocoa, and 1 cup water to a boil in a small saucepan over medium-high, whisking often until butter melts. Add the chocolate, whisking until melted. Whisk the butter mixture into flour mixture until blended. Add the buttermilk, eggs, and vanilla; whisk until blended. Pour the batter into prepared pans.

3. Bake at 350°F for 30 to 35 minutes or until a wooden pick inserted in center comes out clean. Cool in pans on wire racks 10 minutes. Remove from pans. Cool completely on wire racks (about 1 hour). Cut layers in half horizontally.

4. Make the Frosting: Place the butter in a large bowl; beat at medium speed with an electric mixer until creamy. Gradually add the powdered

sugar, beating at low speed until blended. Beat in the vanilla, peppermint extract, and salt. Add the cream; beat at medium speed 1 minute or until smooth. Transfer 2¼ cups of the frosting to a bowl. Stir in the crushed peppermint candies and red food coloring; spread ¾ cup of the frosting between layers. Spread remaining 3¼ cups frosting on top and sides of cake.

5. Make the White Chocolate Snowflakes: Line a baking sheet with parchment paper. Melt the white chocolate in a small microwave-safe bowl on HIGH 1 to 1½ minutes until melted and smooth, stirring at 30-second intervals. Spoon the chocolate into a piping bag fitted with a #3 plain tip. Pipe snowflake patterns onto prepared baking sheet. Refrigerate 30 minutes or until set. Carefully remove from parchment, and place on cake. (Snowflake stencils can also be printed from the Internet.)

Blackberry-Chocolate
Spice Cake

Blackberry-Chocolate Spice Cake

Serves 12 · Hands-on 35 minutes · Total 2 hours 17 minutes

Shortening

Unsweetened cocoa

1 (15.25-ounce) package devil's food cake mix

1 (3.4-ounce) package chocolate instant pudding mix

3 large eggs

1¼ cups milk

1 cup canola oil

1 tablespoon vanilla extract

1 teaspoon chocolate extract

½ teaspoon almond extract

2 teaspoons ground cinnamon

¼ teaspoon ground ginger

¼ teaspoon ground nutmeg

¼ teaspoon ground cloves

2 (3.5-ounce) bittersweet dark chocolate with orange and spices candy bars, chopped

1 (21-ounce) can blackberry pie filling

2 (16-ounce) containers chocolate fudge frosting

Garnish: fresh blackberries

1. Preheat the oven to 350°F. Grease (with shortening) and dust with cocoa 2 (9-inch) round cake pans.

2. Beat the cake mix and next 11 ingredients at low speed with an electric mixer 1 minute; beat at medium speed 2 minutes. Fold in the chopped chocolate. Pour the batter into prepared pans.

3. Bake at 350°F for 30 to 32 minutes or until a wooden pick inserted in center comes out clean. Cool in pans on wire racks 10 minutes. Remove from pans to wire racks, and cool completely (about 1 hour). Wrap cake layers in plastic wrap, and chill at least 1 hour or up to 24 hours.

4. Using a serrated knife, slice cake layers in half horizontally to make 4 layers. Place 1 layer, cut side up, on a cake plate. Spread one-fourth of the blackberry pie filling over cake. Repeat procedure twice. Place the final cake layer on top of cake, cut side down. Spread the chocolate fudge frosting on top and sides of cake. Drizzle remaining filling over top of cake, letting it drip down sides of cake. Cover and chill in refrigerator until ready to serve.

Fresh Strawberry
Meringue Cake

Fresh Strawberry Meringue Cake

Serves 10 to 12 · Hands-on 1 hour · Total 4 hours 20 minutes

Parchment paper
Masking tape
1 cup chopped toasted pecans
2 tablespoons cornstarch
⅛ teaspoon table salt
2 cups sugar
7 large egg whites, at room temperature
½ teaspoon cream of tartar
2 (8-ounce) containers mascarpone cheese
2 teaspoons vanilla extract
3 cups whipping cream
4½ cups sliced fresh strawberries
Halved fresh strawberries

1. Preheat the oven to 250°F. Cover 2 large baking sheets with parchment paper. Draw 2 (8-inch) circles on each sheet of parchment by tracing an 8-inch round cake pan. Turn paper over; secure with masking tape.

2. Process the pecans, cornstarch, salt, and ½ cup of the sugar in a food processor 40 to 45 seconds or until pecans are finely ground.

3. Beat the egg whites and cream of tartar at high speed with an electric mixer until foamy. Gradually add 1 cup of the sugar, 1 tablespoon at a time, beating at medium-high speed until mixture is glossy, stiff peaks form, and sugar dissolves (2 to 4 minutes; do not overbeat). Add half of the pecan mixture to egg white mixture, gently folding just until blended. Repeat procedure with remaining pecan mixture. Gently spoon the egg white mixture onto circles drawn on parchment paper (about 1½ cups mixture per circle), spreading to cover each circle completely.

4. Bake at 250°F for 1 hour, turning baking sheets after 30 minutes. Turn oven off; let meringues stand in closed oven with light on 2 to 2½ hours.

5. Just before assembling cake, stir together the mascarpone cheese and vanilla in a large bowl just until blended. Beat the whipping cream at low speed until foamy; increase speed to medium-high, and gradually add remaining ½ cup sugar, beating until stiff peaks form. (Do not overbeat or cream will be grainy.) Gently fold the whipped cream into mascarpone mixture.

6. Carefully remove 1 meringue from parchment paper; place on a cake plate or serving platter. Spread one-fourth of the mascarpone mixture (about 2 cups) over meringue; top with 1½ cups of the sliced strawberries. Repeat layers 2 times; top with remaining meringue, mascarpone mixture, and halved strawberries. Serve immediately, or chill up to 2 hours. Cut with a sharp, thin-bladed knife.

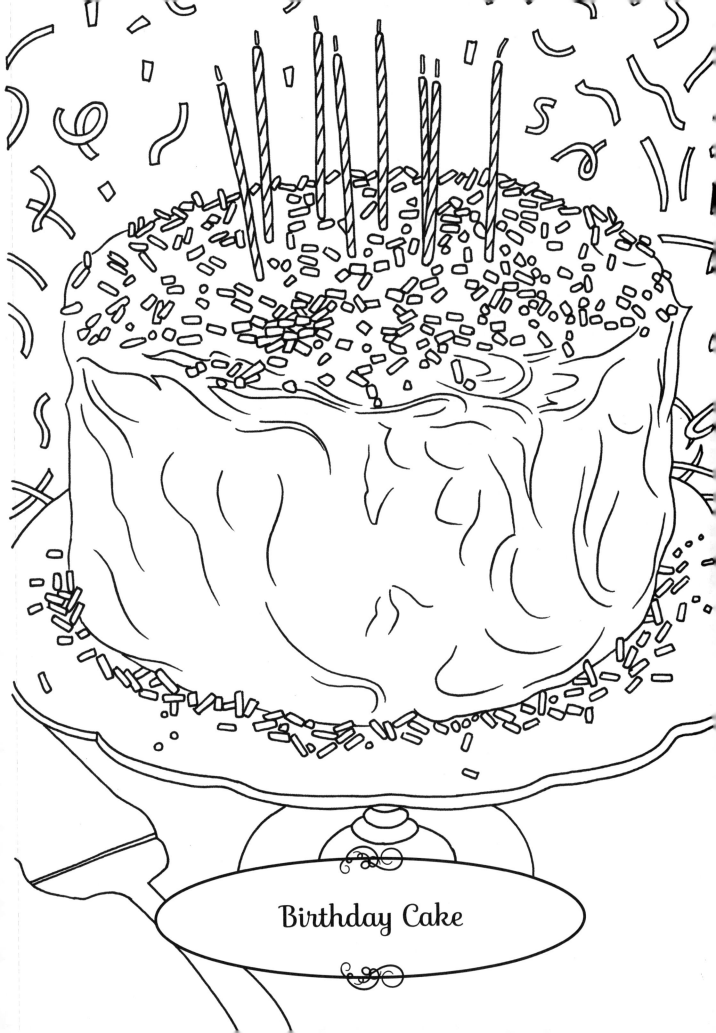

Birthday Cake

Birthday Cake

Serves 12 · Hands-on 15 minutes · Total 7 hours 5 minutes

Cake:

Shortening
- 4 ounces (½ cup) butter, softened
- ½ cup shortening
- 2 cups sugar
- 3 cups (11.3 ounces) cake flour
- 4 teaspoons baking powder
- ½ teaspoon table salt
- ⅔ cup milk
- ⅔ cup water
- 2 teaspoons vanilla extract
- ¾ teaspoon almond extract
- 6 large egg whites

Milk Chocolate Frosting:

- 8 ounces (1 cup) butter, softened
- 6 cups powdered sugar
- ⅓ cup unsweetened cocoa
- ½ cup milk

Garnish: multicolored candy sprinkles

1. Make the Cake: Preheat the oven to 325°F. Grease (with shortening) and flour 3 (8-inch) round cake pans. Beat the butter and shortening at medium speed with an electric mixer until creamy; gradually add sugar, beating well.

2. Combine the flour, baking powder, and salt; add to butter mixture alternately with milk and ⅔ cup water, beginning and ending with flour mixture. Beat at low speed until blended after each addition. Stir in the vanilla and almond extracts.

3. Beat the egg whites at high speed with an electric mixer until stiff peaks form; fold about one-third of the egg whites into batter. Gradually fold in remaining egg whites. Pour the cake batter into prepared pans.

4. Bake at 325°F for 25 to 30 minutes or until a wooden pick inserted in center comes out clean. Cool in pans on wire racks 10 minutes. Remove from pans to wire racks, and cool completely (about 1 hour). Wrap each layer in plastic wrap. Freeze 4 hours.

5. Make the Frosting: Beat the butter at medium speed with an electric mixer until creamy. Add the powdered sugar, cocoa, and milk, beating until smooth. Unwrap frozen cake layers. Spread the Milk Chocolate Frosting between layers and on top and sides of cake. Let stand at room temperature 2 hours before serving.

Peanut Butter-Chocolate Cake

Peanut Butter-Chocolate Cake

Serves 20 · Hands-on 20 minutes · Total 2 hours 25 minutes

Cake:

Shortening

3	cups (12.8 ounces) all-purpose flour
⅓	cup unsweetened dark baking cocoa
1½	teaspoons baking soda
1	teaspoon table salt
1¼	cups firmly packed dark brown sugar
1¼	cups granulated sugar
8	ounces (1 cup) butter, softened
4	large eggs
1	(8-ounce) package semisweet chocolate baking squares, melted and cooled
1½	teaspoons vanilla extract
1⅔	cups buttermilk
1	cup strong brewed coffee, at room temperature

Peanut Butter Frosting:

4	ounces (½ cup) butter, softened
½	cup creamy peanut butter
2	(3-ounce) packages cream cheese, softened
1	(16-ounce) package powdered sugar
1	tablespoon whipping cream
2	teaspoons vanilla extract

Garnish: 12 peanut butter cream-filled chocolate sandwich cookies, chopped

1. Make the Cake: Preheat the oven to 350°F. Grease (with shortening) and lightly flour a 13- x 9-inch pan.

2. Whisk together the flour, cocoa, baking soda, and salt in a medium bowl. Beat the brown sugar, granulated sugar, and butter at medium speed with an electric mixer 2 minutes or until light and fluffy. Add the eggs, 1 at a time, beating until well blended. Add the melted chocolate and vanilla, beating until blended. Add the flour mixture alternately with the buttermilk, beginning and ending with flour mixture. Beat at low speed just until blended after each addition. Beat in the coffee until blended. Pour the batter into prepared pan.

3. Bake at 350°F for 55 to 60 minutes or until a wooden pick inserted in center comes out clean. Cool in pan on a wire rack 10 to 15 minutes; remove from pan to wire rack, and cool completely (about 1 hour).

4. Make the Frosting: Beat the butter, peanut butter, and cream cheese at medium speed with an electric mixer 2 minutes or until blended. Gradually beat in the powdered sugar at low speed until blended. Beat in the whipping cream and vanilla. Spread top of cake with frosting.

Tiramisù Layer Cake

Tiramisù Layer Cake

Serves 10 to 12 · Hands-on 45 minutes · Total 6 hours 40 minutes

Cake:
Shortening
4   ounces (½ cup) butter, softened
½   cup shortening
2   cups sugar
⅔   cup milk
⅔   cup water
3   cups (12.8 ounces) all-purpose
     flour
1   tablespoon baking powder
1   teaspoon table salt
1   tablespoon vanilla bean paste*
1   teaspoon almond extract
6   large egg whites

Coffee Syrup:
1   cup sugar
⅓   cup water
⅔   cup strong brewed coffee
¼   cup brandy

Mascarpone Frosting:
2   (3-ounce) packages cream
     cheese, softened
4   ounces (½ cup) butter, softened
10⅔ cups powdered sugar
2   (8-ounce) packages mascarpone
     cheese
4   teaspoons vanilla extract

Garnishes: raspberries, strawberries,
     red currants, fresh mint

1. Make the Cake: Preheat the oven to 350°F. Grease (with shortening) and flour 3 (8-inch) round cake pans. Beat the butter and ½ cup shortening at medium speed with an electric mixer until fluffy; gradually add sugar, beating well.

2. Stir together the milk and ⅔ cup water. Combine the flour and next 2 ingredients; add to butter mixture alternately with milk mixture, beginning and ending with flour mixture. Beat at low speed just until blended after each addition. Stir in the vanilla bean paste and almond extract.

3. Beat the egg whites at high speed until stiff peaks form, and fold into batter. Spoon the batter into prepared pans.

4. Bake at 350°F for 25 to 30 minutes or until a wooden pick inserted in center comes out clean. Cool in pans on wire racks 10 minutes; remove from pans to wire racks, and cool completely (about 1 hour).

5. Make the Syrup: Combine the sugar and ⅓ cup water in a microwave-safe bowl. Microwave at HIGH 1½ minutes or until sugar is dissolved, stirring

at 30-second intervals. Stir in coffee and brandy. Cool 1 hour. Pierce the cake layers with a wooden pick, making holes 1 inch apart. Brush or spoon the Coffee Syrup over layers.

6. Make the Frosting: Beat the cream cheese and butter at medium speed with an electric mixer until creamy; gradually add powdered sugar, beating at low speed until blended after each addition. Add the mascarpone cheese and vanilla, beating until blended. Place 1 cake layer, brushed side up, on a cake stand or serving plate. Spread top with 1⅓ cups of the Mascarpone Frosting. Top with second cake layer, brushed side up, and spread with 1⅓ cups of the frosting. Top with remaining cake layer, brushed side up. Spread top and sides of cake with remaining frosting. Chill 4 hours before serving.

*Vanilla extract may be substituted for vanilla bean paste.

Chocolate Marble Sheet Cake

Chocolate Marble Sheet Cake

Serves 12 · Hands-on 20 minutes · Total 1 hour 43 minutes

Cake:

Shortening

8	ounces (1 cup) butter, softened
1¾	cups sugar
2	large eggs
2	teaspoons vanilla extract
2½	cups (10.6 ounces) all-purpose flour
1	tablespoon baking powder
½	teaspoon table salt
1	cup half-and-half
¼	cup unsweetened cocoa
3	tablespoons hot water

Mocha Frosting:

3	cups powdered sugar
⅔	cup unsweetened cocoa
3	tablespoons hot coffee
2	teaspoons vanilla extract
4	ounces (½ cup) butter, softened

3 to 4 tablespoons half-and-half

1. Make the Cake: Preheat the oven to 325°F. Grease (with shortening) and flour a 15- x 10-inch jelly-roll pan. Beat the butter and 1½ cups of the sugar at medium speed with a heavy-duty electric stand mixer 4 to 5 minutes or until creamy. Add the eggs, 1 at a time, beating just until blended after each addition. Beat in the vanilla.

2. Sift together the flour, baking powder, and salt. Add to the butter mixture alternately with half-and-half, beginning and ending with flour mixture. Beat at low speed just until blended after each addition, stopping to scrape bowl as needed.

3. Spoon 1¼ cups of the batter into a 2-quart bowl, and stir in cocoa, 3 tablespoons hot water, and remaining ¼ cup sugar until well blended.

4. Spread remaining vanilla batter into prepared pan. Spoon the chocolate batter onto vanilla batter in pan; gently swirl with a knife or small spatula.

5. Bake at 325°F for 23 to 28 minutes or until a wooden pick inserted in center comes out clean. Cool completely in pan on a wire rack (about 1 hour).

6. Make the Frosting: Whisk together the powdered sugar and unsweetened cocoa in a medium bowl. Combine the hot coffee and vanilla. Beat the butter at medium speed with a heavy-duty electric stand mixer until creamy; gradually add sugar mixture alternately with coffee mixture, beating at low speed until blended. Beat in the half-and-half, 1 tablespoon at a time, until smooth and desired spreading consistency. Spread top of cake with frosting.

Strawberry Shortcake

Strawberry Shortcake

Serves 8 · Hands-on 30 minutes · Total 2 hours 8 minutes

2 (16-ounce) containers fresh strawberries, sliced
¼ to ½ cup granulated sugar
4 ounces (½ cup) butter, softened
2 cups (8.5 ounces) all-purpose flour
1 tablespoon plus 1 teaspoon baking powder
¼ teaspoon table salt
¼ cup granulated sugar
Dash of ground nutmeg
½ cup milk
2 large eggs, separated
¼ cup granulated sugar
1 cup whipping cream
¼ cup powdered sugar
Garnishes: sliced fresh strawberries, fresh mint leaves

1. Combine the sliced strawberries and desired amount of granulated sugar; stir gently, and chill 1 to 2 hours. Drain, reserving syrup for another use.

2. Preheat the oven to 450°F. Butter 2 (9-inch) round cake pans with ½ teaspoon of the butter each. Combine the flour and next 4 ingredients in a large bowl; cut in remaining butter with a pastry blender until mixture is crumbly.

3. Whisk together the milk and egg yolks. Add to the flour mixture; stir with a fork until a soft dough forms. Pat the dough out into prepared cake pans. (Dough will be sticky; moisten fingers with water as necessary.)

4. Beat the egg whites at medium speed with an electric mixer just until stiff peaks form. Brush surface of dough with beaten egg white; sprinkle with ¼ cup granulated sugar.

5. Bake at 450°F for 8 to 10 minutes or until layers are golden brown. (Layers will be thin.) Remove from pans to wire racks, and cool completely (about 30 minutes).

6. Beat the whipping cream until foamy; gradually add powdered sugar, beating until soft peaks form. Place 1 cake layer on a serving plate. Spread half of the whipped cream over layer, and arrange half of the sweetened strawberries on top. Repeat procedure with remaining layer, whipped cream, and sweetened strawberries, reserving a small amount of whipped cream. Top the cake with remaining whipped cream. Store in refrigerator.

Pink Lemonade Cake

Pink Lemonade Cake

Serves 15 · Hands-on 35 minutes · Total 2 hours 15 minutes

Cake:
Shortening
2¾ cups (11.7 ounces) all-purpose flour
1⅔ cups granulated sugar
1 cup milk
6 ounces (¾ cup) butter, softened
½ cup presweetened pink lemonade flavor drink mix (from 19-ounce container)
3 teaspoons baking powder
2 teaspoons vanilla extract
1 teaspoon lemon zest
¼ teaspoon table salt
4 large egg whites
1 whole large egg

Pink Lemonade Frosting:
¼ cup presweetened pink lemonade flavor drink mix
3 tablespoons water
½ cup butter, softened
1 tablespoon whipping cream
1 teaspoon lemon zest
1 (16-ounce) package powdered sugar
1 to 2 tablespoons whipping cream

Garnishes: pink decorating sugar, edible pink pearls

1. Make the Cake: Preheat the oven to 350°F. Grease (with shortening) and lightly flour a 13- x 9-inch pan.

2. Beat the flour and next 8 ingredients at low speed with an electric mixer 30 seconds, scraping down sides as needed. Beat at high speed 2 minutes, scraping down sides as needed. Beat in the egg whites and egg at high speed 2 minutes, scraping down sides as needed. Pour the batter into prepared pan.

3. Bake at 350°F for 35 to 45 minutes or until a wooden pick inserted in center comes out clean. Cool in pan on a wire rack 10 to 15 minutes; remove from pan to wire rack, and cool completely (about 1 hour).

4. Make the Frosting: Stir lemonade flavor drink mix in 3 tablespoons water until dissolved. Beat the butter, whipping cream, lemon zest, and lemonade mixture at low speed with an electric mixer 30 seconds or until creamy. Gradually add the powdered sugar, beating at low speed until blended. Gradually beat in 1 to 2 tablespoons whipping cream, 1 teaspoon at a time, until smooth and desired spreading consistency. Spread top of cake with frosting.

White Chocolate-
Cranberry Cheesecake

White Chocolate-Cranberry Cheesecake

Serves 6 to 8 · Hands-on 35 minutes · Total 12 hours 40 minutes

Cheesecake:

Shortening
1 (9-ounce) package chocolate wafer cookies
½ (4-ounce) semisweet chocolate baking bar, chopped
4 ounces (½ cup) butter, melted
¼ cup sugar
1 (6-ounce) package white chocolate baking bar, chopped
¼ cup whipping cream
2 (8-ounce) packages cream cheese, softened
2 tablespoons all-purpose flour
⅓ cup sugar
4 large eggs
½ cup chopped sweetened dried cranberries
½ (4-ounce) semisweet chocolate baking bar, finely chopped
¼ cup amaretto liqueur

Cranberry Topping:

1 (12-ounce) package fresh cranberries
1 cup sugar
¼ cup water
½ cup seedless raspberry jam

Garnish: fresh mint leaves

1. Make the Cheesecake: Preheat the oven to 350°F. Lightly grease (with shortening) a 10-inch pie plate. Pulse the wafer cookies and chopped semisweet chocolate in a food processor 8 to 10 times or until mixture resembles fine crumbs. Stir together the crumb mixture, melted butter, and ¼ cup sugar; firmly press on bottom, up sides, and onto lip of prepared pie plate. Bake at 350°F for 10 minutes. Transfer to a wire rack, and cool completely (about 30 minutes). Reduce oven temperature to 325°F.

2. Microwave the white chocolate and whipping cream at MEDIUM (50% power) 1 to 1½ minutes or until melted and smooth, stirring at 30-second intervals.

3. Beat the cream cheese, flour, and ⅓ cup sugar at medium speed with an electric mixer 1 minute or until creamy and smooth. Add the eggs, 1 at a time, beating just until blended after each addition. Add the cranberries, next 2 ingredients, and white chocolate mixture. Beat at low speed just until blended. Spoon the batter into prepared crust.

4. Bake at 325°F for 30 to 35 minutes or until set. Cool completely on a wire rack (about 2 hours). Cover and chill 8 hours.

5. Make the Topping: Bring the cranberries, sugar, and ¼ cup water to a boil in a 3-quart saucepan over medium-high, stirring often. Boil, stirring often, 6 to 8 minutes or until mixture thickens to a syrup-like consistency. Remove from heat, and stir in the jam. Cool completely (about 1 hour). Cover and chill 8 hours. Spoon the Cranberry Topping over pie before serving.

Mississippi Mud Cheesecake

Mississippi Mud Cheesecake

Serves 16 · Hands-on 20 minutes · Total 9 hours

Vegetable cooking spray

24 thin chocolate wafer cookies (from 9-ounce package), crushed (about 1⅔ cups)

⅓ cup finely chopped pecans

2 tablespoons sugar

3 ounces (6 tablespoons) butter, melted

4 (8-ounce) packages cream cheese, softened

1¼ cups sugar

2 tablespoons all-purpose flour

1 teaspoon vanilla extract

4 large eggs

2 (4-ounce) semisweet chocolate baking bars, melted and cooled

2 cups miniature marshmallows

½ cup chopped toasted pecans

½ cup ready-to-spread chocolate frosting (from 16-ounce container)

1. Preheat the oven to 300°F. Wrap outside bottom and sides of a 9-inch springform pan with heavy-duty foil to prevent leaking. Lightly spray inside bottom and sides of pan with cooking spray. Combine the cookie crumbs and next 3 ingredients in a bowl with a pastry blender until crumbly. Press the mixture into bottom of pan. Bake at 300°F for 12 minutes or until set. Cool crust on a wire rack 10 minutes.

2. Meanwhile, beat the cream cheese, 1¼ cups sugar, flour, and vanilla at medium speed with an electric mixer until light and fluffy. Add the eggs, 1 at a time, beating just until blended. Add the melted chocolate, beating until blended. Pour over crust.

3. Bake at 300°F for 1 hour and 15 minutes or until almost set. Turn oven off. Let cheesecake stand in oven, with oven door open at least 4 inches, for 30 minutes. Remove from oven, and gently run a knife around outer edge of cheesecake to loosen from sides of pan. (Do not remove sides of pan.) Sprinkle with the marshmallows. Cool on a wire rack 30 minutes. Sprinkle with the pecans.

4. Microwave the frosting in a small microwave-safe bowl at HIGH 15 seconds or until pourable. Drizzle the frosting over marshmallows and pecans. Refrigerate at least 6 hours or overnight.

5. To serve, gently run small metal spatula around edge of pan to loosen; carefully remove foil and sides of pan.

Chocolate Fudge Cheesecakes

Chocolate Fudge Cheesecakes

Serves 20 · Hands-on 30 minutes · Total 10 hours 36 minutes

Cheesecakes:

½ cup finely chopped toasted pecans

Shortening

1 (4-ounce) unsweetened chocolate baking bar

8 ounces (1 cup) butter, softened

3¾ cups sugar

11 large eggs, divided

1 cup (4.25 ounces) all-purpose flour

1 cup semisweet chocolate morsels

3 teaspoons vanilla extract

4 (8-ounce) packages cream cheese, softened

Chocolate Glaze:

1 (12-ounce) package semisweet chocolate morsels

½ cup whipping cream

Garnish: chocolate-dipped pecan halves

1. Make the Cheesecakes: Preheat the oven to 325°F. Sprinkle the toasted pecans over bottoms of 2 greased (with shortening) and floured 9-inch springform pans.

2. Microwave the chocolate baking bar in a microwave-safe bowl at MEDIUM (50% power) 1½ minutes or until melted and smooth, stirring at 30-second intervals.

3. Beat the butter and 2 cups of the sugar at medium speed with an electric mixer until light and fluffy. Add 4 of the eggs, 1 at a time, beating just until blended after each addition. Add the melted chocolate, beating just until blended. Add the flour, beating at low speed just until blended. Stir in the chocolate morsels and 1 teaspoon of the vanilla. Divide the batter between pans, spreading to edges of pan over chopped pecans.

4. Beat the cream cheese at medium speed until smooth; add remaining 1¾ cups sugar, beating until blended. Add remaining 7 eggs, 1 at a time, beating just until blended after each addition. Stir in remaining 2 teaspoons vanilla. Divide the cream cheese mixture between each pan, spreading over chocolate batter.

5. Bake at 325°F for 1 hour or until set. Remove from oven, and gently run a knife around outer edge of cheesecake to loosen from sides of pan. (Do not remove sides of pan.) Cool on wire racks 1 hour or until completely cool.

6. Make the Glaze: Melt the chocolate morsels and whipping cream in a 2-quart microwave-safe bowl at MEDIUM (50% power) 2½ to 3 minutes or until chocolate begins to melt, stirring at 1-minute intervals. Whisk until the chocolate is melted and mixture is smooth. Spread tops of cooled cheesecakes with the Chocolate Glaze; cover and chill 8 hours. Remove sides of pans.

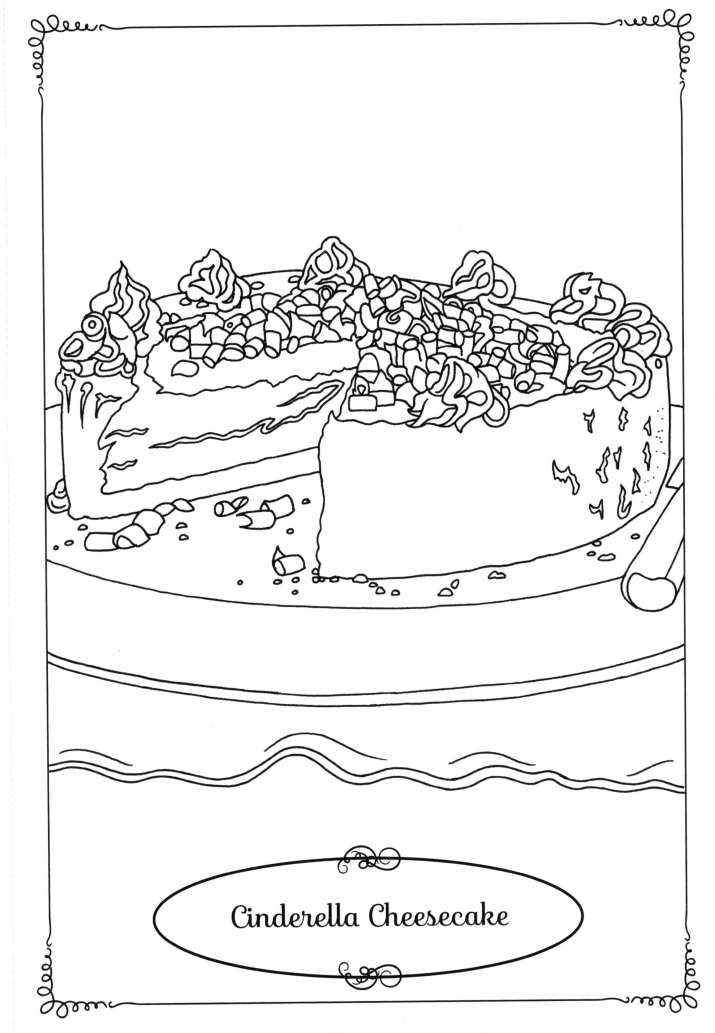

Cinderella Cheesecake

Cinderella Cheesecake

Serves 10 to 12 · Hands-on 45 minutes · Total 11 hours 5 minutes

Cheesecake:

Shortening

3 (1-ounce) unsweetened chocolate baking squares

2 ounces (¼ cup) unsalted butter

½ cup (2.1 ounces) sifted all-purpose flour

⅛ teaspoon table salt

⅛ teaspoon baking powder

2 large eggs

1 cup firmly packed light brown sugar

1½ teaspoons vanilla extract

½ (1-ounce) bittersweet chocolate baking square, finely chopped

1½ (8-ounce) packages cream cheese, softened

1 cup firmly packed light brown sugar

3 large eggs

½ cup sour cream

1⅓ cups creamy peanut butter

Sour Cream Topping:

¾ cup sour cream

2 teaspoons sugar

Chocolate curls

Peanut butter

1. Make the Cheesecake: Preheat the oven to 350°F. Grease (with shortening) and flour a 9-inch springform pan. Microwave the chocolate squares and butter in a small microwave-safe bowl at MEDIUM (50% power) 1½ minutes or until melted and smooth, stirring at 30-second intervals. Stir together the flour, salt, and baking powder in a bowl.

2. Beat 2 eggs and 1 cup brown sugar at medium-high speed with an electric mixer 3 to 4 minutes or until batter forms thin ribbons when beaters are lifted. Add the vanilla, bittersweet chocolate, and melted chocolate mixture, and beat just until blended. Stir in the flour mixture just until combined.

3. Spread 1 cup of the brownie mixture on bottom of prepared pan. Bake at 350°F on center oven rack 13 to 15 minutes or until set. Cool on a wire rack 10 minutes; freeze 15 minutes. Remove from freezer; spread remaining brownie batter up sides of pan to ¼ inch from top, sealing batter to bottom crust.

4. Beat the cream cheese and 1 cup brown sugar at medium speed with a heavy-duty electric stand mixer until blended. Add 3 eggs, 1 at a time, beating just until yellow disappears after each addition. Beat in the sour cream just until blended. Beat in the peanut butter until blended. Pour the filling into prepared crust. (Mixture will not completely fill crust.) Bake at 350°F for 35 minutes or until center is almost set. Remove from oven.

5. Make the Topping: Stir together the sour cream and sugar in a small bowl until smooth. Spread the Sour Cream Topping over center of cheesecake, leaving a 2-inch border around edge. Bake at 350°F for 1 more minute. Remove from oven, and gently run a knife around outer edge of cheesecake to loosen from sides of pan. (Do not remove sides of pan.) Cool completely on a wire rack.

6. Cover and chill 8 to 12 hours. Remove sides of pan. Top with chocolate curls, and pipe peanut butter around edge.

Toffee S'mores Cheesecake

Toffee S'mores Cheesecake

Serves 16 · Hands-on 30 minutes · Total 9 hours

Vegetable cooking spray
2 cups graham cracker crumbs
3 ounces (6 tablespoons) butter, melted
3 (8-ounce) packages cream cheese, softened
1 cup sugar
1 teaspoon vanilla extract
3 large eggs
6 ounces semisweet baking chocolate, melted and cooled
1 cup sour cream
5 (1.4-ounce) chocolate-covered toffee candy bars, coarsely chopped
7 large marshmallows

1. Preheat the oven to 325°F. Wrap outside bottom and sides of 9-inch springform pan with heavy-duty foil to prevent leaking. Lightly spray inside bottom and sides of pan with cooking spray. Combine the crumbs and melted butter in a medium bowl. Press in bottom and halfway up sides of pan. Bake at 325°F for 10 minutes or until set. Cool crust 10 minutes.

2. Beat the cream cheese, sugar, and vanilla at medium speed with an electric mixer until smooth. Beat in the eggs, 1 at a time, just until blended after each addition. Divide batter evenly between 2 bowls. Beat melted chocolate into 1 bowl; stir in ¾ cup of the sour cream. Beat remaining ¼ cup sour cream into second bowl; stir in chopped toffee candy bars. Pour the toffee batter over crust. Carefully spread with chocolate batter.

3. Bake at 325°F for 1 hour and 15 minutes or until almost set. Turn oven off. Let cheesecake stand in oven, with oven door open at least 4 inches, for 30 minutes. Remove from oven, and gently run a knife around outer edge of cheesecake to loosen from sides of pan. (Do not remove sides of pan.) Cool on a wire rack 30 minutes. Refrigerate at least 6 hours or overnight.

4. Just before serving, run a small metal spatula around edge of pan; carefully remove foil and sides of pan. Set oven control to broil. Place cheesecake on a baking sheet. Cut marshmallows in half horizontally with dampened kitchen scissors. Place marshmallows, cut side down, on top of cheesecake. Broil about 6 inches from heat 1 to 2 minutes or until golden brown.

White Chocolate-
Raspberry Cheesecake

White Chocolate-Raspberry Cheesecake

Serves 12 · Hands-on 22 minutes · Total 9 hours 20 minutes

Shortening
2 cups graham cracker crumbs
3 tablespoons sugar
4 ounces (½ cup) butter, melted
5 (8-ounce) packages cream cheese, softened
1 cup sugar

2 large eggs
1 tablespoon vanilla extract
1 (12-ounce) package white chocolate morsels, melted and slightly cooled
¾ cup raspberry preserves
Garnish: fresh raspberries

1. Preheat the oven to 350°F. Lightly grease (with shortening) a 9-inch springform pan. Combine the graham cracker crumbs and next 2 ingredients; press crumb mixture into bottom of prepared pan. Bake at 350°F for 8 minutes; cool slightly.

2. Beat the cream cheese at medium speed with an electric mixer until creamy; gradually add 1 cup sugar, beating well. Add the eggs, 1 at a time, beating until blended after each addition. Stir in the vanilla. Add the melted white chocolate, beating well.

3. Microwave the raspberry preserves in a small microwave-safe bowl at HIGH 30 seconds to 1 minute or until melted; stir well.

4. Spoon half of the cream cheese batter into prepared crust; spread a little more than half of the melted preserves over batter, leaving a ¾-inch border. Spoon remaining cream cheese batter around edges of pan, spreading toward center. Cover remaining raspberry preserves, and chill.

5. Bake at 350°F for 50 minutes or until cheesecake is just set and slightly browned. Remove from oven, and gently run a knife around outer edge of cheesecake to loosen from sides of pan. (Do not remove sides of pan.) Cool completely on a wire rack. Cover and chill at least 8 hours.

6. Reheat remaining preserves briefly in microwave to melt. Pour the preserves over top of cheesecake, leaving a 1-inch border. Remove sides of pan.

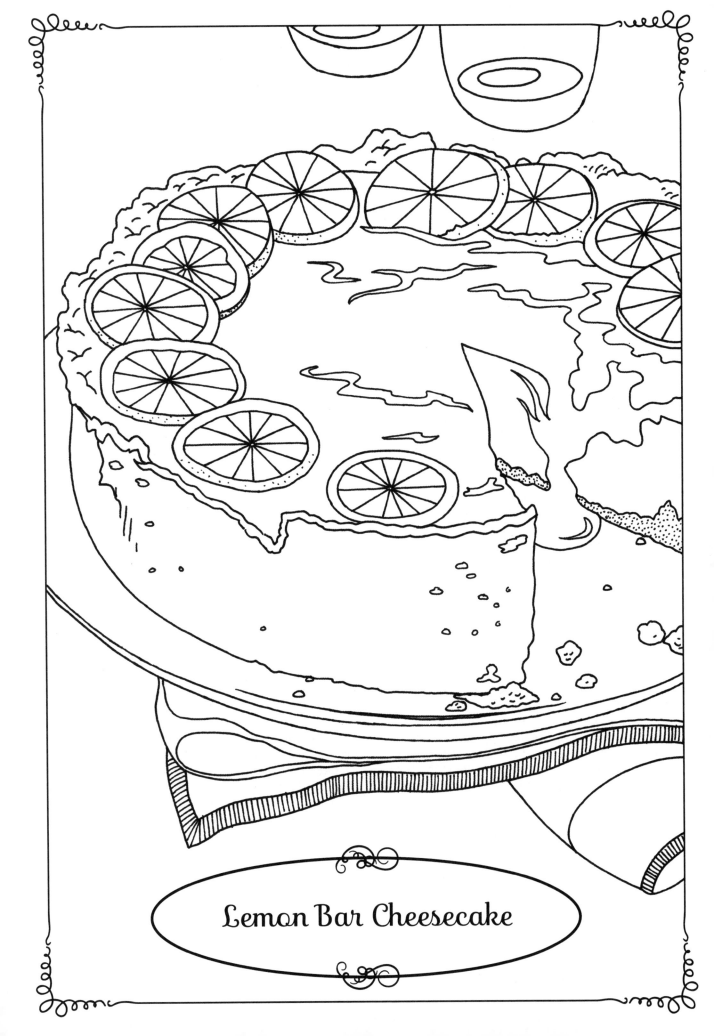

Lemon Bar Cheesecake

Lemon Bar Cheesecake

Serves 10 to 12 · Hands-on 40 minutes · Total 22 hours 45 minutes

Cheesecake:

- 2 cups (8.5 ounces) all-purpose flour
- ½ cup powdered sugar
- ¼ teaspoon table salt
- 4 ounces (½ cup) cold butter, cubed
- 2 large egg yolks
- 1 to 2 tablespoons ice-cold water
- Shortening
- 4 (8-ounce) packages cream cheese, softened
- 1 cup granulated sugar
- 4 large eggs
- 2 teaspoons vanilla extract

Quick and Easy Lemon Curd:

- 6 lemons
- 1 cup lemon juice
- 4 ounces (½ cup) butter, softened
- 2 cups sugar
- 4 large eggs

Candied Lemon Slices (optional):

- 1 cup sugar
- 2 tablespoons fresh lemon juice
- ¾ cup water
- 2 small lemons, cut into ⅛-inch-thick rounds, seeds removed

1. Make the Cheesecake: Pulse the first 3 ingredients in a food processor 3 or 4 times or just until blended. Add the butter, and pulse 5 or 6 times or until crumbly. Whisk together the egg yolks and 1 tablespoon of the ice-cold water in a small bowl; add to butter mixture, and process until dough forms a ball and pulls away from sides of bowl, adding up to 1 tablespoon remaining ice-cold water, 1 teaspoon at a time, if necessary. Shape the dough into a disk; wrap in plastic wrap. Chill 4 to 24 hours.

2. Roll dough into a 14-inch circle on a lightly floured surface. Fit dough into a lightly greased (with shortening) 9-inch dark springform pan, gently pressing on bottom and up sides of pan; trim and discard excess dough. Chill 30 minutes.

3. Meanwhile, preheat the oven to 325°F. Beat the cream cheese at medium speed with an electric mixer 3 minutes or until smooth. Gradually add the granulated sugar, beating until blended. Add the eggs, 1 at a time, beating just until yellow disappears after each addition. Beat in the vanilla. Pour two-thirds of the cheesecake batter (about 4 cups) into prepared crust; dollop 1 cup of the lemon curd over batter in pan, and gently swirl with a knife. Spoon remaining batter into pan.

4. Bake at 325°F for 1 hour to 1 hour and 10 minutes or just until center is set. Turn oven off. Let the cheesecake stand in oven, with door closed, 15 minutes. Remove from oven, and gently run a knife around outer edge of cheesecake to loosen from sides of pan. (Do not remove sides of pan.) Cool completely in pan on a wire rack (about 1 hour). Cover and chill 8 to 24 hours.

5. Make the Curd: Grate the zest from the lemons to equal 2 tablespoons. Cut the lemons in half; squeeze juice into a measuring cup to equal 1 cup.

6. Beat the butter and sugar at medium speed with an electric mixer until blended. Add the eggs, 1 at a time, beating just until blended after each addition. Gradually add the lemon juice to butter mixture, beating at low speed just until blended after each addition; stir in zest. (Mixture will look curdled.) Transfer to a 3-quart microwave-safe bowl. Microwave at HIGH 5 minutes, stirring at 1-minute intervals. Microwave, stirring at 30-second intervals, 1 to 2 more minutes or until mixture thickens, coats the back of a spoon, and starts to mound slightly when stirred. Place plastic wrap directly on warm curd (to prevent a film from forming), and chill 4 hours or until firm. Store in an airtight container in refrigerator up to 2 weeks.

7. Make the Slices: Stir together the sugar, lemon juice, and ¾ cup water in a large skillet over medium until sugar is dissolved. Add the lemon slices, and simmer gently, keeping slices in a single layer and turning occasionally, 14 to 16 minutes or until slightly translucent and rinds are softened. Remove from heat. Place the slices in a single layer in a wax paper-lined jelly-roll pan, using tongs. Cool completely (about 1 hour). Cover and chill 2 hours to 2 days. Store syrup in refrigerator, and reserve for another use.

8. Remove sides of pan, and transfer cheesecake to a serving platter. Spoon remaining 1 cup lemon curd over cheesecake, and, if desired, top with Candied Lemon Slices.

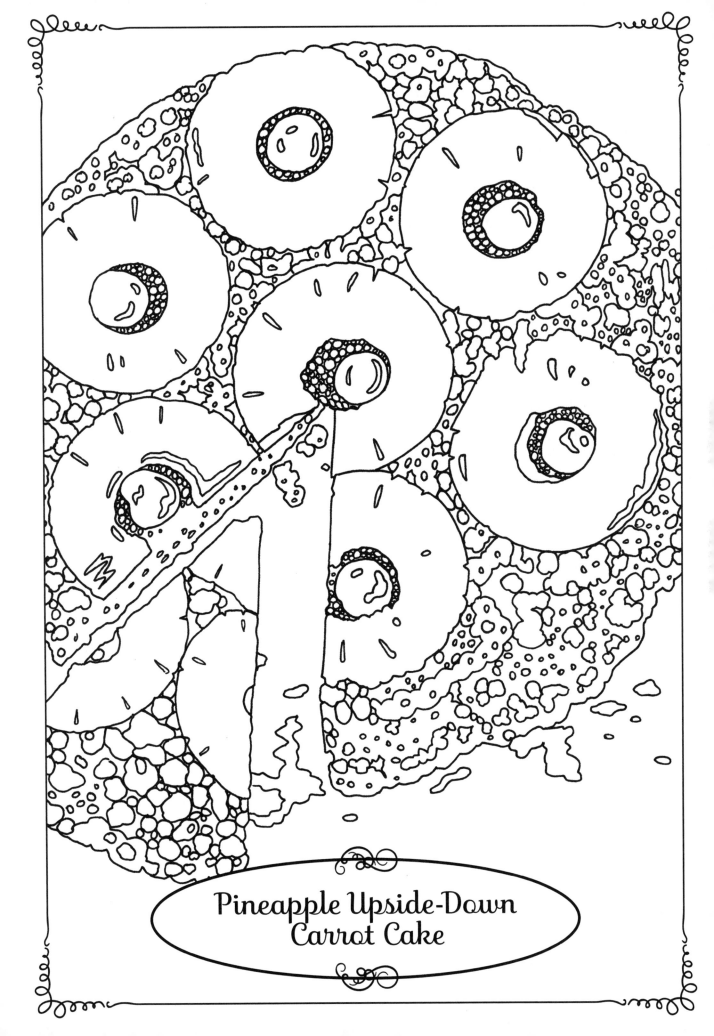

Pineapple Upside-Down
Carrot Cake

Pineapple Upside-Down Carrot Cake

Serves 8 · Hands-on 30 minutes · Total 1 hour 15 minutes

Shortening
2 ounces (¼ cup) butter
⅔ cup firmly packed brown sugar
1 (20-ounce) can pineapple slices in juice, drained
7 maraschino cherries (without stems)
1 cup granulated sugar
½ cup vegetable oil

2 large eggs
1 cup (4.3 ounces) all-purpose flour
1 teaspoon baking powder
1 teaspoon ground cinnamon
¾ teaspoon baking soda
½ teaspoon table salt
1½ cups grated carrots
½ cup finely chopped pecans

1. Preheat the oven to 350°F. Lightly grease (with shortening) a 10-inch cast-iron skillet or 9-inch round cake pan (with sides that are at least 2 inches high). Melt the butter in prepared pan over low. Remove from heat. Sprinkle with the brown sugar. Arrange 7 of the pineapple slices in a single layer over brown sugar, reserving remaining pineapple slices for another use. Place 1 cherry in center of each pineapple slice.

2. Beat the granulated sugar, oil, and eggs at medium speed with an electric mixer until blended. Combine the flour and next 4 ingredients; gradually add to sugar mixture, beating at low speed just until blended. Stir in the carrots and pecans. Spoon the batter over pineapple slices.

3. Bake at 350°F for 45 to 50 minutes or until a wooden pick inserted in center comes out clean. Cool in skillet on a wire rack 10 minutes. Carefully run a knife around edge of cake to loosen. Invert cake onto a serving plate, spooning any topping in skillet over cake.

Pound Cake from Heaven

Pound Cake from Heaven

Serves 12 · Hands-on 15 minutes · Total 3 hours 30 minutes

Shortening

12 ounces (1½ cups) unsalted butter, softened

3 cups sugar

5 large eggs

3 cups (12.8 ounces) all-purpose soft-wheat flour

1 teaspoon baking powder

¼ teaspoon table salt

1 (5-ounce) can evaporated milk

⅔ cup heavy cream

1 tablespoon vanilla extract

Garnishes: sweetened whipped cream, fresh strawberries

1. Preheat the oven to 350°F. Grease (with shortening) and flour a 10-inch (16-cup) tube pan. Place the butter in the bowl of a heavy-duty electric stand mixer, and beat at medium speed until light and fluffy (about 6 minutes). Gradually add the sugar, beating until blended. Beat 1 more minute. Add the eggs, 1 at a time, beating just until yellow disappears after each addition.

2. Combine the flour and next 2 ingredients. Combine the evaporated milk and cream; add to butter mixture alternately with flour mixture, beginning and ending with flour mixture. Beat at low speed just until blended after each addition, stopping to scrape down sides as needed. Stir in the vanilla. Pour the batter into prepared pan.

3. Bake at 350°F for 1 hour and 15 minutes or until a long wooden pick inserted in center comes out clean. Cool in pan on a wire rack 1 hour; remove from pan to wire rack, and cool completely (about 1 hour).

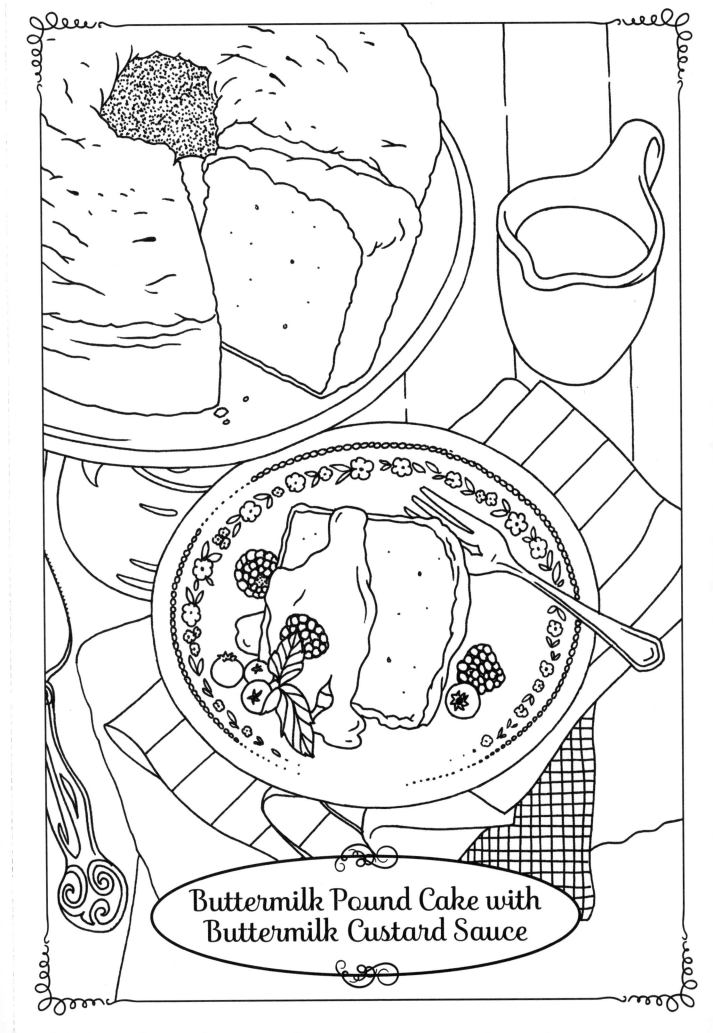

Buttermilk Pound Cake with Buttermilk Custard Sauce

Buttermilk Pound Cake with Buttermilk Custard Sauce

Serves 12 · Hands-on 15 minutes · Total 2 hours 45 minutes

Cake:

Shortening

10½ ounces (1⅓ cups) butter, softened

2½ cups sugar

6 large eggs

3 cups (12.8 ounces) all-purpose flour

½ cup buttermilk

1 teaspoon vanilla extract

Buttermilk Custard Sauce:

2 cups buttermilk

½ cup sugar

1 tablespoon cornstarch

3 large egg yolks

1 teaspoon vanilla extract

Garnishes: blueberries, raspberries, mint sprigs

1. Make the Cake: Preheat the oven to 325°F. Grease (with shortening) and flour a 10-inch (16-cup) tube pan. Beat the butter at medium speed with a heavy-duty electric stand mixer until creamy. Gradually add the sugar, beating at medium speed until light and fluffy. Add the eggs, 1 at a time, beating just until blended after each addition.

2. Add the flour to butter mixture alternately with buttermilk, beginning and ending with flour. Beat at low speed just until blended after each addition. Stir in the vanilla. Pour the batter into prepared pan.

3. Bake at 325°F for 1 hour and 5 minutes to 1 hour and 10 minutes or until a long wooden pick inserted in center comes out clean. Cool in pan on a wire rack 10 to 15 minutes; remove from pan to wire rack, and cool completely (about 1 hour).

4. Make the Sauce: Whisk together the buttermilk, sugar, cornstarch, and egg yolks in a heavy 3-quart saucepan. Bring to a boil over medium, whisking constantly, and boil 1 minute. Remove from heat, and stir in vanilla. Serve cake with warm or cold Buttermilk Custard Sauce. Store leftovers in an airtight container in refrigerator for up to 1 week.

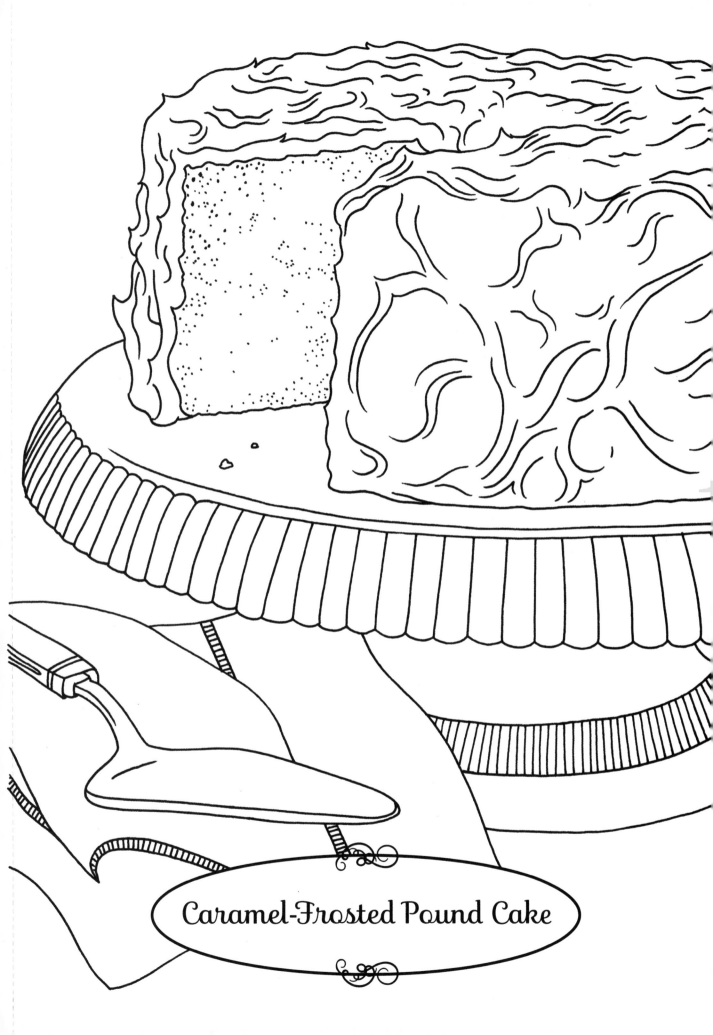

Caramel-Frosted Pound Cake

Caramel-Frosted Pound Cake

Serves 16 · Hands-on 45 minutes · Total 4 hours

Cake:

Shortening

3	cups sugar
8	ounces (1 cup) butter, softened
6	large eggs
2	teaspoons vanilla extract
1	teaspoon almond extract
3	cups (12.8 ounces) all-purpose flour
1	cup whipping cream

Caramel Frosting:

¼	cup sugar
1¼	cups sugar
½	cup butter
½	cup milk

1. Make the Cake: Preheat the oven to 325°F. Grease (with shortening) and flour a 10-inch (16-cup) tube pan.

2. Beat the sugar and butter at medium speed with an electric mixer 5 minutes or until light and fluffy. Add the eggs, 1 at a time, beating well after each addition. Beat in the vanilla and almond extracts. Add the flour alternately with whipping cream, beginning and ending with flour, beating well after each addition. Beat at medium speed 2 minutes. Pour the batter into prepared pan.

3. Bake at 325°F for 1 hour and 15 minutes or until a long wooden pick inserted in center comes out clean. Cool in pan on a wire rack 10 to 15 minutes; remove from pan to wire rack, and cool completely (about 1 hour).

4. Make the Frosting: Heat ¼ cup sugar in an 8- or 10-inch skillet over medium until amber colored, about 6 minutes, shaking pan occasionally (do not stir). Meanwhile, heat 1¼ cups sugar, butter, and milk in a 3-quart saucepan to boiling over medium-high. Gradually stir in the caramelized sugar with a whisk; cook until a candy thermometer registers 232°F. Remove from heat; cool, about 20 minutes, stirring occasionally, until frosting is smooth and spreadable. Using an offset spatula and working quickly, spread the Caramel Frosting over cake (frosting will harden as it cools). Let stand 30 minutes before slicing.

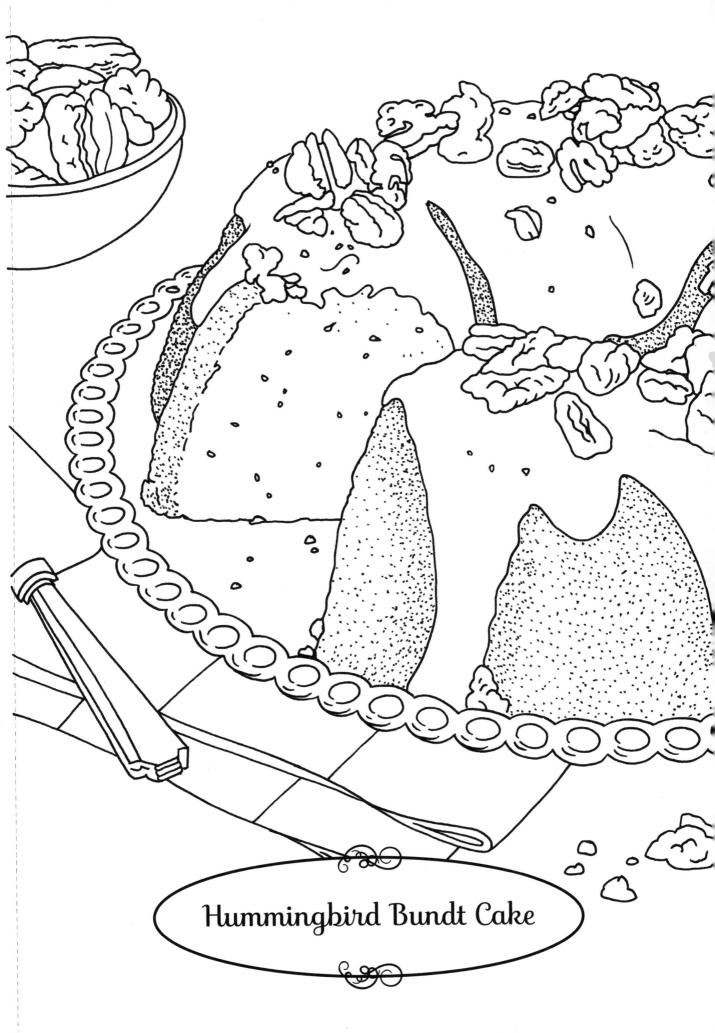

Hummingbird Bundt Cake

Hummingbird Bundt Cake

Serves 10 to 12 · Hands-on 20 minutes · Total 3 hours 45 minutes

Cake:

Shortening
1½ cups chopped toasted pecans
3 cups (12.8 ounces) all-purpose flour
2 cups sugar
1 teaspoon baking soda
1 teaspoon ground cinnamon
½ teaspoon table salt
3 large eggs, lightly beaten
1¾ cups mashed ripe bananas (about 4 large)
1 (8-ounce) can crushed pineapple, undrained
¾ cup canola oil
1½ teaspoons vanilla extract

Cream Cheese Glaze:

4 ounces cream cheese, softened
2 cups sifted powdered sugar
1 teaspoon vanilla extract
2 tablespoons milk

1. Make the Cake: Preheat the oven to 350°F. Grease (with shortening) and flour a 10-inch (12-cup) Bundt pan. Sprinkle 1 cup of the toasted pecans into prepared pan. Stir together the flour and next 4 ingredients in a large bowl; stir in eggs and next 4 ingredients, stirring just until dry ingredients are moistened. Spoon the batter over pecans.

2. Bake at 350°F for 1 hour to 1 hour and 10 minutes or until a long wooden pick inserted in center comes out clean. Cool the cake in pan on a wire rack 15 minutes; remove from pan to wire rack, and cool completely (about 2 hours).

3. Make the Glaze: Process the cream cheese, powdered sugar, vanilla, and 1 tablespoon of the milk in a food processor until well blended. Add remaining 1 tablespoon milk, 1 teaspoon at a time, processing until smooth. Immediately pour glaze over cooled cake, and sprinkle with remaining ½ cup toasted pecans.

Tennessee Jam Bundt

Tennessee Jam Bundt

Serves 12 · Hands-on 30 minutes · Total 4 hours 30 minutes

Cake:

Shortening

1½	cups sugar
8	ounces (1 cup) butter, softened
4	large eggs
3	cups (12.8 ounces) all-purpose flour
2	tablespoons unsweetened cocoa
1	teaspoon ground cinnamon
½	teaspoon table salt
½	teaspoon ground allspice
¼	teaspoon ground nutmeg
1	cup buttermilk
1	teaspoon baking soda
1½	cups seedless blackberry jam
2	teaspoons vanilla extract
1½	cups chopped toasted pecans

Caramel Glaze:

½	cup firmly packed dark brown sugar
½	cup whipping cream
2	ounces (¼ cup) butter
1	teaspoon vanilla extract
1¼	cups powdered sugar

Garnishes: fresh mint sprigs, blackberries

1. Make the Cake: Preheat the oven to 325°F. Grease (with shortening) and flour a 12-cup Bundt pan. Beat the granulated sugar and butter at medium speed with a heavy-duty electric stand mixer until light and fluffy. Add the eggs, 1 at a time, beating just until blended after each addition.

2. Stir together the flour and next 5 ingredients. Stir together the buttermilk and baking soda. Add the flour mixture to butter mixture alternately with buttermilk mixture, beginning and ending with flour mixture. Beat at low speed just until blended after each addition. Add the jam and vanilla, and beat just until blended. Stir in pecans. Pour the batter into prepared pan.

3. Bake at 325°F for 1 hour to 1 hour and 15 minutes or until a long wooden pick inserted in center comes out clean. Cool cake in pan on a wire rack 20 minutes; remove from pan to wire rack, and cool completely (about 2 hours).

4. Make the Glaze: Bring the brown sugar, whipping cream, and butter to a boil in a 2-quart saucepan over medium, whisking constantly; boil, whisking constantly, 1 minute. Remove from heat; stir in vanilla. Gradually whisk in powdered sugar until smooth. Gently stir 3 to 5 minutes or until mixture begins to cool and thicken. Immediately pour the Caramel Glaze over cooled cake.

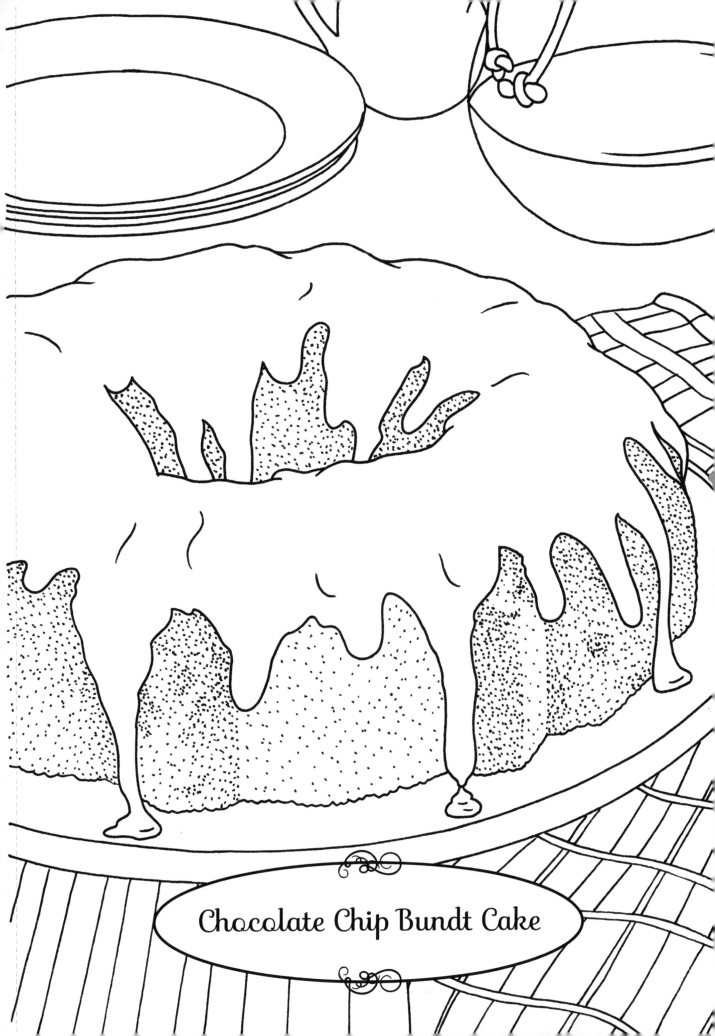

Chocolate Chip Bundt Cake

Chocolate Chip Bundt Cake

Serves 12 · Hands-on 25 minutes · Total 2 hours 25 minutes

Cake:
Shortening
⅔ cup chopped pecans
2 ounces (¼ cup) butter, softened
2 tablespoons granulated sugar
2¾ cups (11.7 ounces) all-purpose flour
1 teaspoon baking soda
1 teaspoon table salt
8 ounces (1 cup) butter, softened
1 cup firmly packed dark brown sugar
½ cup granulated sugar
1 tablespoon vanilla extract
4 large eggs
1 cup buttermilk
1 (12-ounce) package semisweet chocolate mini-morsels

Powdered Sugar Glaze:
1 cup powdered sugar
4 tablespoons heavy cream
½ teaspoon vanilla extract

1. **Make the Cake:** Preheat the oven to 350°F. Grease (with shortening) and flour a 10-inch (12-cup) Bundt pan. Stir together pecans and next 2 ingredients in a small bowl, using a fork. Sprinkle into prepared pan.

2. Whisk together the flour, baking soda, and salt.

3. Beat the butter, brown sugar, granulated sugar, and vanilla at medium speed with a heavy-duty electric stand mixer 3 to 5 minutes or until fluffy. Add the eggs, 1 at a time, beating just until blended. Add the flour mixture alternately with buttermilk, beginning and ending with flour mixture. Beat at low speed just until blended after each addition, stopping to scrape down sides as needed. Beat in chocolate mini-morsels. (Mixture will be thick.) Spoon the batter into prepared pan.

4. Bake at 350°F for 50 to 55 minutes or until a long wooden pick inserted in center comes out clean. Cool in pan on a wire rack 10 minutes; remove from pan to wire rack, and cool completely (about 1 hour).

5. **Make the Glaze:** Stir together the powdered sugar, heavy cream, and vanilla to desired consistency. Drizzle the cake with the Powdered Sugar Glaze.

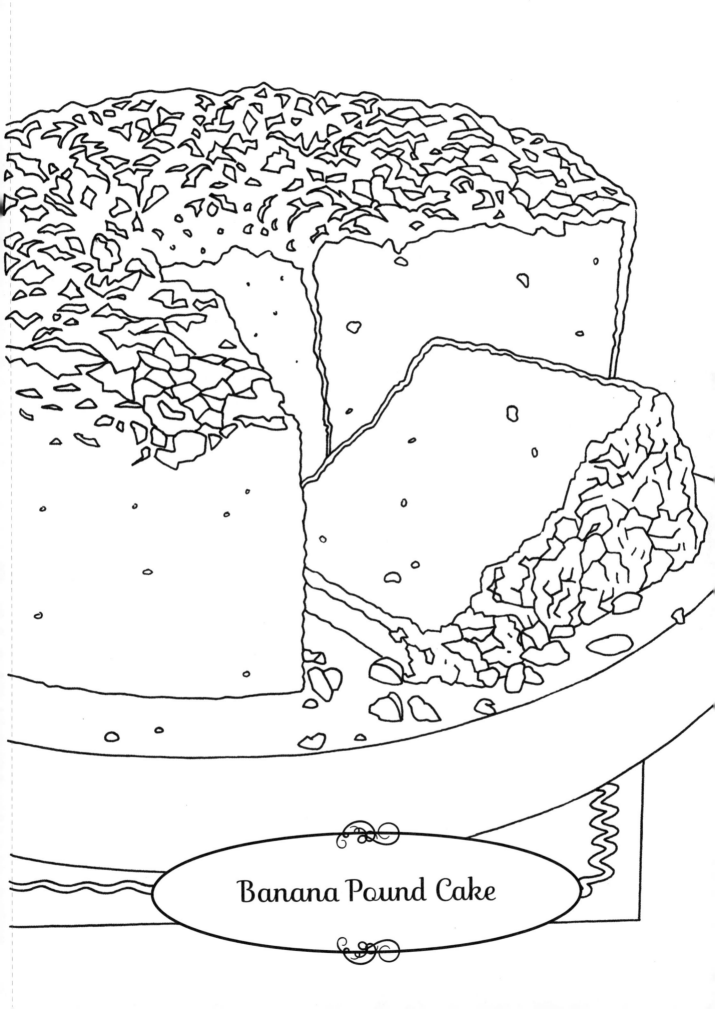

Banana Pound Cake

Banana Pound Cake

Serves 10 to 12 · **Hands-on** 18 minutes · Total 2 hours 48 minutes

Shortening
12 ounces (1½ cups) butter, softened
3 cups sugar
5 large eggs
3 ripe bananas, mashed
3 tablespoons milk

2 teaspoons vanilla extract
3 cups (12.8 ounces) all-purpose flour
1 teaspoon baking powder
½ teaspoon table salt
¾ cup chopped pecans

1. Preheat the oven to 350°F. Grease (with shortening) and flour a 10-inch (16-cup) tube pan. Beat the butter at medium speed with an electric mixer about 2 minutes or until creamy. Gradually add the sugar, beating 5 to 7 minutes. Add the eggs, 1 at a time, beating just until yellow disappears after each addition.

2. Combine the mashed bananas, milk, and vanilla.

3. Combine the flour, baking powder, and salt; add to batter alternately with banana mixture, beginning and ending with flour mixture. Beat at low speed just until blended after each addition. Pour into prepared pan. Sprinkle with the pecans.

4. Bake at 350°F for 1 hour and 20 minutes or until a long wooden pick inserted in center comes out clean. Cool in pan on a wire rack 10 to 15 minutes. Remove from pan to wire rack, and cool completely (about 1 hour).

Banana Split Cake

Banana Split Cake

Serves 10 to 12 · Hands-on 30 minutes · Total 2 hours 40 minutes

Shortening
3 cups (12.8 ounces) all-purpose flour
2 cups sugar
1 teaspoon baking soda
¼ teaspoon table salt
3 large eggs
1 cup vegetable oil
½ cup buttermilk
2 cups mashed banana (5 medium)
1 cup chopped pecans
1 cup sweetened flaked coconut
1½ teaspoons vanilla extract
1 (20-ounce) can crushed pineapple, undrained
1 (16-ounce) jar maraschino cherries, drained
1 (8-ounce) package cream cheese, softened
1½ cups powdered sugar
Garnishes: grated milk chocolate, chopped pecans, hot fudge sauce, maraschino cherries with stems, toasted sweetened flaked coconut

1. Preheat the oven to 350°F. Grease (with shortening) and flour a 10-inch (16-cup) tube pan. Combine the flour and next 3 ingredients in a large bowl. Stir together the eggs, oil, and buttermilk. Add the oil mixture to flour mixture, stirring just until dry ingredients are moistened. Stir in the banana and next 3 ingredients.

2. Drain pineapple, reserving 2 tablespoons liquid. Gently press pineapple and maraschino cherries between layers of paper towels. Chop cherries. Stir pineapple and cherries into banana mixture. Spoon into prepared pan.

3. Bake at 350°F for 1 hour or until a long wooden pick inserted in center comes out clean. Cool in pan on a wire rack 10 to 15 minutes. Remove from pan to wire rack, and cool completely (about 1 hour).

4. Beat the cream cheese at medium speed with an electric mixer until smooth. Gradually add the powdered sugar, beating at low speed until blended. Stir in the reserved pineapple juice. Pour over the cake.

Cranberry-Apple-
Pumpkin Bundt

Cranberry-Apple-Pumpkin Bundt

Serves 12 · Hands-on 30 minutes · Total 4 hours 30 minutes

Cake:

Shortening
1½ cups peeled and diced Granny Smith apples
2 tablespoons butter, melted
½ cup finely chopped sweetened dried cranberries
½ cup firmly packed light brown sugar
3 tablespoons all-purpose flour
¾ cup finely chopped toasted pecans
2 cups granulated sugar
8 ounces (1 cup) butter, softened
4 large eggs
1 (15-ounce) can pumpkin
1 tablespoon vanilla extract
3 cups (12.8 ounces) all-purpose flour
2 teaspoons baking powder
2 teaspoons pumpkin pie spice
½ teaspoon baking soda

Maple Glaze:

½ cup pure maple syrup
2 tablespoons butter
1 tablespoon milk
1 teaspoon vanilla extract
1 cup powdered sugar

Sugared Pecans and Pepitas:

1 cup pecan halves and pieces
½ cup roasted, salted, shelled pepitas (pumpkin seeds)
2 tablespoons butter, melted
2 tablespoons sugar

1. Make the Cake: Preheat the oven to 325°F. Grease (with shortening) and flour a 10-inch (12-cup) Bundt pan. Toss the diced apples in 2 tablespoons melted butter to coat in a medium bowl; add cranberries and next 3 ingredients, and toss until well blended.

2. Beat the granulated sugar and 1 cup butter at medium speed with an electric mixer until light and fluffy. Add the eggs, 1 at a time, beating just until blended after each addition. Add the pumpkin and vanilla; beat just until blended.

3. Stir together 3 cups flour and next 3 ingredients. Gradually add the flour mixture to butter mixture, beating at low speed just until blended after each addition. Spoon half of the batter into prepared pan. Spoon the apple mixture over batter, leaving a ½-inch border around outer edge. Spoon remaining batter over apple mixture.

4. Bake at 325°F for 1 hour and 10 minutes to 1 hour and 20 minutes or until a long wooden pick inserted in center comes out clean. Cool in pan on a wire rack 15 minutes. Remove from pan to wire rack; cool completely (about 2 hours).

5. Make the Glaze: Bring the maple syrup, butter, and 1 tablespoon milk to a boil in a small saucepan over medium-high, stirring constantly; boil, stirring constantly, 2 minutes. Remove from heat; whisk in vanilla. Gradually whisk in the powdered sugar until smooth; stir gently 3 to 5 minutes or until mixture begins to thicken and cool slightly.

6. Make the Sugared Pecans and Pepitas: Preheat the oven to 350°F. Stir together the pecans, pepitas (pumpkin seeds), and melted butter. Spread in a single layer in a 13- x 9-inch pan. Bake at 350°F for 12 to 15 minutes or until toasted, stirring halfway through. Remove from oven; toss with the sugar. Cool completely in pan on a wire rack.

7. Spoon the Maple Glaze immediately onto cooled cake. Arrange the Sugared Pecans and Pepitas on cake.

Apple-Cream Cheese Bundt Cake

Apple-Cream Cheese Bundt Cake

Serves 12 · Hands-on 40 minutes · Total 4 hours 10 minutes

Cake:

Shortening

3 cups (12.8 ounces) all-purpose flour

1 cup granulated sugar

1 cup firmly packed light brown sugar

2 teaspoons ground cinnamon

1 teaspoon table salt

1 teaspoon baking soda

1 teaspoon ground nutmeg

½ teaspoon ground allspice

3 large eggs, lightly beaten

¾ cup canola oil

¾ cup applesauce

1 teaspoon vanilla extract

3 cups peeled and finely chopped Gala apples (about 1½ pounds)

1 cup finely chopped toasted pecans

Cream Cheese Filling:

1 (8-ounce) package cream cheese, softened

2 ounces (¼ cup) butter, softened

½ cup granulated sugar

1 large egg

2 tablespoons all-purpose flour

1 teaspoon vanilla extract

Praline Frosting:

½ cup firmly packed brown sugar

2 ounces (¼ cup) butter

3 tablespoons milk

1 teaspoon vanilla extract

1 cup powdered sugar

Garnish: chopped toasted pecans

1. Make the Cake: Preheat the oven to 350°F. Grease (with shortening) and flour a 10-inch (12-cup) Bundt pan. Stir together 3 cups flour and next 7 ingredients in a large bowl; stir in eggs and next 3 ingredients, stirring just until dry ingredients are moistened. Stir in the apples and 1 cup pecans.

2. Make the Filling: Beat the cream cheese, butter, and sugar at medium speed with an electric mixer until blended and smooth. Add the egg, flour, and vanilla; beat just until blended.

3. Spoon two-thirds of the apple mixture into prepared pan. Spoon the Cream Cheese Filling over apple mixture, leaving a 1-inch border around edges of pan. Swirl the filling through apple mixture using a paring knife. Spoon remaining apple mixture over filling.

4. Bake at 350°F for 1 hour to 1 hour and 15 minutes or until a long wooden pick inserted in center comes out clean. Cool the cake in pan on a wire rack 15 minutes; remove from pan to wire rack, and cool completely (about 2 hours).

5. Make the Frosting: Bring the sugar, butter, and milk to a boil in a 2-quart saucepan over medium heat, whisking constantly; boil 1 minute, whisking constantly. Remove from heat; stir in vanilla. Gradually whisk in powdered sugar until smooth; stir gently 3 to 5 minutes or until mixture begins to cool and thickens slightly. As soon as the Praline Frosting is made, pour immediately over cooled cake.

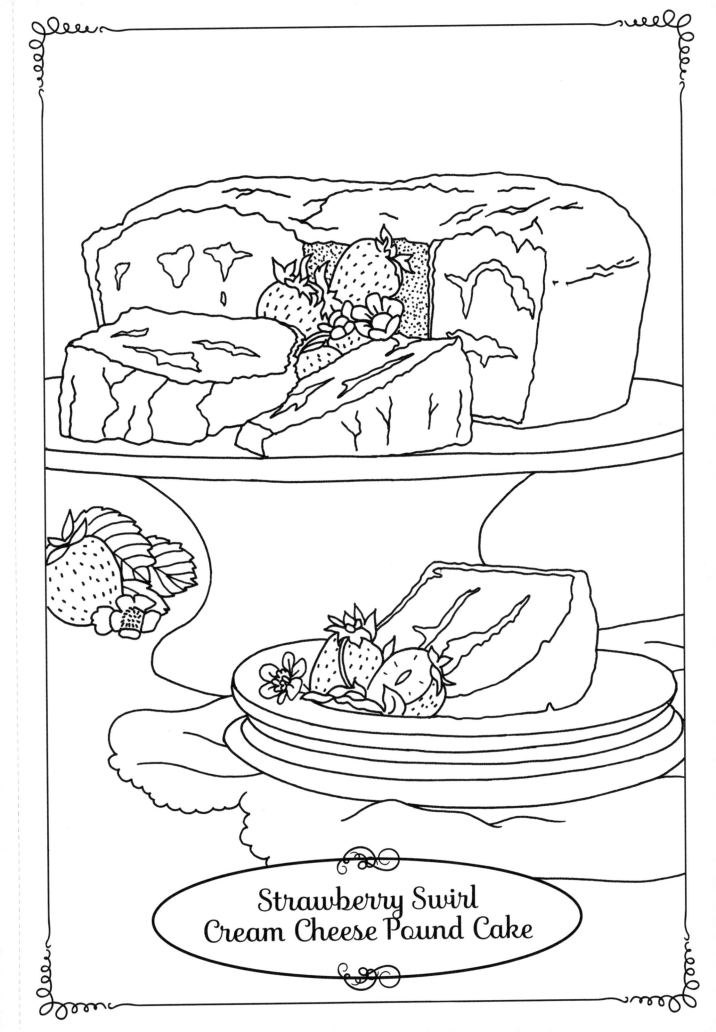

Strawberry Swirl
Cream Cheese Pound Cake

Strawberry Swirl Cream Cheese Pound Cake

Serves 12 · Hands-on 25 minutes · Total 2 hours 35 minutes

Shortening
12 ounces (1½ cups) butter, softened
3   cups sugar
1   (8-ounce) package cream cheese, softened
6   large eggs
3   cups (12.8 ounces) all-purpose flour

1   teaspoon almond extract
½   teaspoon vanilla extract
⅔   cup strawberry glaze
1   (6-inch) wooden skewer
Garnishes: fresh strawberries, fresh mint leaves

1. Preheat the oven to 350°F. Grease (with shortening) and flour a 10-inch (16-cup) tube pan. Beat the butter at medium speed with a heavy-duty electric stand mixer until creamy. Gradually add the sugar, beating at medium speed until light and fluffy. Add the cream cheese, beating until creamy. Add the eggs, 1 at a time, beating just until blended after each addition.

2. Gradually add the flour to butter mixture. Beat at low speed just until blended after each addition, stopping to scrape bowl as needed. Stir in the almond and vanilla extracts. Pour one-third of the batter into prepared pan (about 2⅔ cups batter). Dollop 8 rounded teaspoonfuls strawberry glaze over batter, and swirl with wooden skewer. Repeat procedure once, and top with remaining third of batter.

3. Bake at 350°F for 1 hour to 1 hour and 10 minutes or until a long wooden pick inserted in center comes out clean. Cool in pan on a wire rack 10 to 15 minutes; remove from pan to wire rack, and cool completely (about 1 hour).

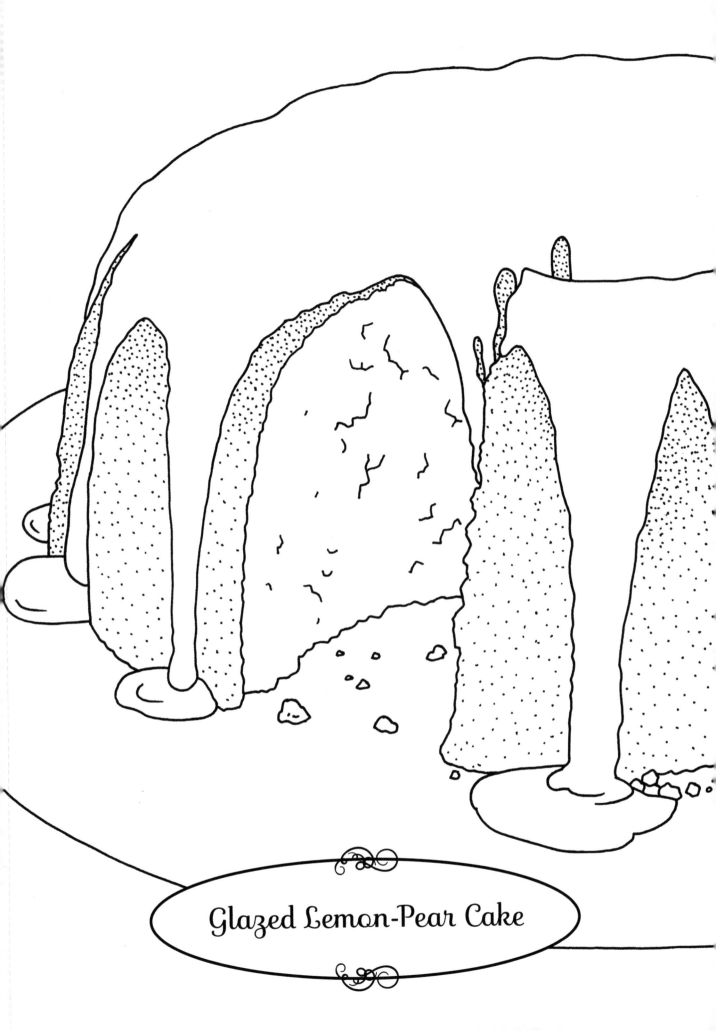

Glazed Lemon-Pear Cake

Glazed Lemon-Pear Cake

Serves 16 · Hands-on 20 minutes · Total 2 hours 30 minutes

Cake:

Shortening

3¾ cups (16 ounces) all-purpose flour

3 teaspoons baking powder

½ teaspoon ground allspice

¼ teaspoon table salt

10 ounces (1¼ cups) butter, softened

1¾ cups sugar

5 large eggs

1¼ cups milk

1 cup shredded peeled pears

1 cup finely chopped toasted walnuts

¾ teaspoon lemon zest

Poured Lemon Frosting:

2 cups powdered sugar

¾ teaspoon lemon zest

2 tablespoons fresh lemon juice

1. Make the Cake: Preheat the oven to 350°F. Grease (with shortening) and lightly flour a 10-inch (12-cup) Bundt pan (do not use cooking spray).

2. Combine the flour, baking powder, allspice, and salt in a medium bowl. Beat the butter and sugar at low speed with an electric mixer 30 seconds, scraping down sides as needed. Beat at high speed 3 minutes, scraping down sides as needed, until light and fluffy. Add the eggs, 1 at a time, beating well after each addition. Add the flour mixture alternately with milk, beating at low speed just until blended after each addition, beginning and ending with flour mixture. Fold in the pears, walnuts, and lemon zest. Pour the batter into prepared pan.

3. Bake at 350°F for 1 hour or until a long wooden pick inserted in center comes out clean. Cool in pan on a wire rack 10 to 15 minutes; remove from pan to wire rack, and cool completely (about 1 hour).

4. Make the Frosting: Whisk together the powdered sugar, lemon zest, and lemon juice, 1 teaspoon at a time, for desired consistency. Spoon the Poured Lemon Frosting over cake, allowing some to drizzle down sides.

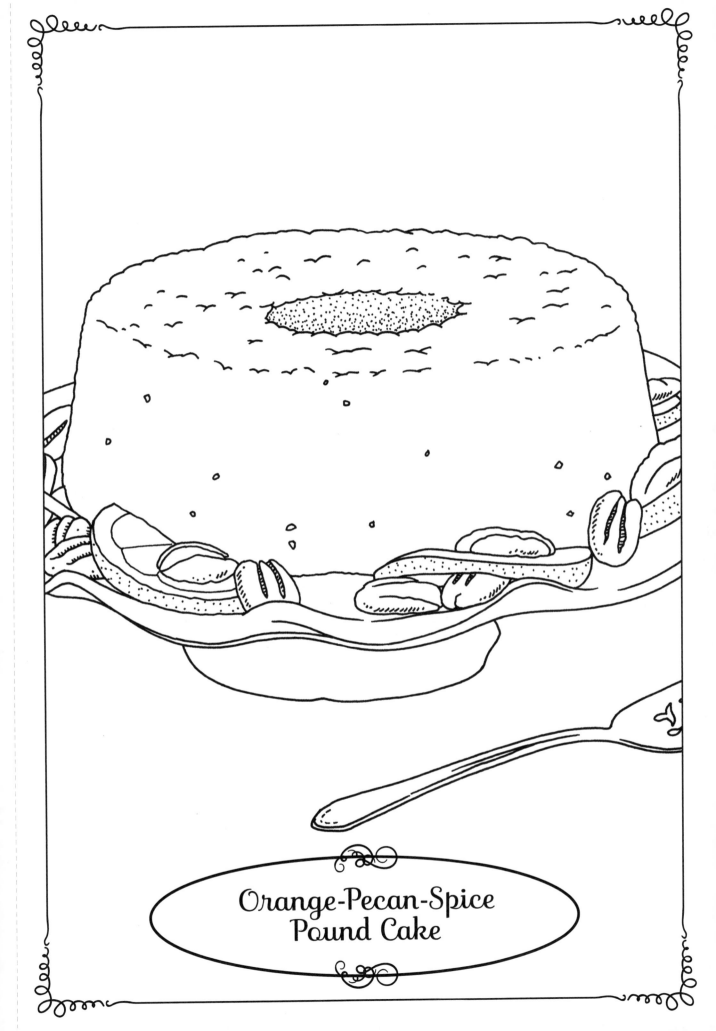

Orange-Pecan-Spice
Pound Cake

Orange-Pecan-Spice Pound Cake

Serves 10 to 12 · Hands-on 35 minutes · Total 3 hours 35 minutes

Cake:

Butter
- 2 cups finely chopped toasted pecans
- 16 ounces (2 cups) butter, softened
- 3 cups sugar
- 6 large eggs
- 4 cups (17 ounces) all-purpose flour
- ⅛ teaspoon table salt
- ¾ cup milk
- 2 tablespoons orange zest
- 2 teaspoons ground cinnamon
- 1 teaspoon ground nutmeg
- 1 teaspoon vanilla extract
- 1 teaspoon lemon extract
- 1 teaspoon orange extract
- ½ teaspoon ground cloves

Orange Syrup:

- 1 large orange
- 1 cup sugar

Garnishes: pecan halves, halved orange slices

1. Make the Cake: Preheat the oven to 300°F. Grease (with butter) a 10-inch (16-cup) tube pan. Sprinkle 1¼ cups of the toasted pecans into prepared pan; shake to evenly coat bottom and sides of pan.

2. Beat 2 cups butter at medium speed with an electric mixer until creamy; gradually add sugar, beating well. Add the eggs, 1 at a time, beating until blended after each addition.

3. Combine the flour and salt; add to butter mixture alternately with milk, beginning and ending with flour mixture. Beat at low speed until blended after each addition. Stir in the orange zest, next 6 ingredients, and remaining ¾ cup pecans. Spoon the batter into prepared pan.

4. Bake at 300°F for 1 hour and 30 minutes to 1 hour and 40 minutes or until a long wooden pick inserted in center comes out clean. Cool in pan on a wire rack 20 minutes. Remove cake from pan; invert cake, pecan crust side up, onto wire rack.

5. Make the Syrup: Remove the zest from orange with a vegetable peeler, being careful not to get the bitter white pith. Squeeze the orange to get ½ cup juice. Combine the orange zest, juice, and sugar in a small saucepan. Cook over low, stirring until sugar dissolves. Bring mixture to a boil over medium-high, and boil 2 minutes. Brush the top and sides of pound cake gently several times with the hot Orange Syrup, allowing the cake to absorb the syrup after each brushing. (Do not pour syrup over the cake.) Cool the cake completely (about 1 hour).

Green Tea-Honeysuckle Cake

Green Tea-Honeysuckle Cake

Serves 12 · Hands-on 30 minutes · Total 3 hours 15 minutes

Cake:
Shortening
8 ounces (1 cup) butter, softened
½ cup shortening
2½ cups sugar
¼ cup honey
6 large eggs
3 cups (12.8 ounces) all-purpose flour
1 teaspoon baking powder
½ teaspoon table salt
¾ cup milk
2 teaspoons matcha (green tea powder)

Honeysuckle Glaze:
¾ cup sugar
4 ounces (½ cup) butter
⅓ cup honey
⅓ cup orange liqueur
3 tablespoons water

1. **Make the Cake:** Preheat the oven to 325°F. Grease with shortening and flour a 10-inch (12-cup) Bundt pan. Beat the butter and ½ cup shortening at medium speed with a heavy-duty electric stand mixer until creamy. Gradually add the sugar, beating until light and fluffy. Add the honey, beating until blended. Add eggs, 1 at a time, beating just until blended after each addition.

2. Stir together the flour and next 2 ingredients. Add to the butter mixture alternately with milk, beginning and ending with flour mixture. Beat at low speed just until blended after each addition. Transfer 2½ cups of the batter to a 2-quart bowl, and stir in matcha until blended.

3. Drop 2 scoops of the plain batter into prepared pan, using a small cookie scoop (about 1½ inches); top with 1 scoop of the matcha batter. Repeat procedure around entire pan, covering bottom completely. Continue layering the batters in pan as directed until all batter is used.

4. Bake at 325°F for 1 hour and 5 minutes to 1 hour and 15 minutes or until a long wooden pick inserted in center comes out clean. Remove the cake from oven.

5. **Make the Glaze:** Bring the sugar, butter, honey, orange liqueur, and 3 tablespoons water to a boil in a 1-quart saucepan over medium, stirring often; reduce heat to medium-low, and boil, stirring constantly, 3 minutes. Spoon 1 cup of the hot Honeysuckle Glaze over cake in pan, allowing glaze to soak into cake after each addition. Reserve remaining glaze. Cool cake completely in pan on a wire rack (about 1 hour and 30 minutes). Remove cake from pan; spoon reserved glaze over cake.

Coffee Cake Pound Cake

Coffee Cake Pound Cake

Serves 12 · Hands-on 30 minutes · Total 3 hours

Cake:
Shortening
8 ounces (1 cup) butter, softened
2½ cups granulated sugar
6 large eggs
3 cups (12.8 ounces) all-purpose flour
¼ teaspoon baking soda
1 (8-ounce) container sour cream
2 teaspoons vanilla extract
1 cup finely chopped toasted pecans
¼ cup firmly packed brown sugar
1½ teaspoons ground cinnamon

Pecan Streusel:
½ cup firmly packed brown sugar
½ cup (2.1 ounces) all-purpose flour
1 teaspoon ground cinnamon
2 ounces (¼ cup) butter
¾ cup chopped pecans

1. Make the Cake: Preheat the oven to 325°F. Grease (with shortening) and flour a 10-inch (16-cup) tube pan. Beat the butter at medium speed with a heavy-duty electric stand mixer until creamy. Gradually add the granulated sugar, beating until light and fluffy. Add the eggs, 1 at a time, beating just until blended after each addition.

2. Stir together the flour and baking soda; add to butter mixture alternately with sour cream, beginning and ending with flour mixture. Beat at low speed just until blended after each addition. Stir in the vanilla.

3. Pour half of the batter into prepared pan. Stir together the toasted pecans, brown sugar, and cinnamon; sprinkle over batter. Spoon remaining batter over pecan mixture.

4. Make the Streusel: Combine the brown sugar, flour, and ground cinnamon in a bowl. Cut in the butter with a pastry blender until crumbly. Stir in the chopped pecans. Sprinkle the batter with the Pecan Streusel.

5. Bake at 325°F for 1 hour and 20 minutes to 1 hour and 30 minutes or until a long wooden pick inserted in center comes out clean. Cool in pan on a wire rack 10 to 15 minutes; remove from pan to wire rack, and cool completely (about 1 hour).

Maryland Black Walnut Cake

Maryland Black Walnut Cake

Serves 12 · Hands-on 20 minutes · Total 2 hours 30 minutes

Shortening
1½ cups chopped black walnuts
8 ounces (1 cup) butter, softened
1½ cups granulated sugar
3 large eggs, separated
1 teaspoon vanilla extract
2 cups (8.5 ounces) all-purpose flour
1 tablespoon baking powder
¼ teaspoon table salt
¾ cup milk
¼ cup powdered sugar
Vanilla ice cream (optional)
Sliced fresh strawberries (optional)
Chopped black walnuts (optional)

1. Preheat the oven to 350°F. Grease (with shortening) and flour a 10-inch (12-cup) Bundt pan. Pulse 1½ cups black walnuts in a food processor 8 to 10 times or until finely ground.

2. Beat the butter at medium speed with an electric mixer until creamy; gradually add granulated sugar, beating until light and fluffy. Add the egg yolks and vanilla, beating just until blended.

3. Sift together the flour, baking powder, and salt; add to butter mixture alternately with milk, beginning and ending with flour mixture. Beat the batter at low speed just until blended after each addition.

4. Beat the egg whites at medium speed with an electric mixer until stiff peaks form; fold into batter. Fold the ground walnuts into batter. Spoon the batter evenly into prepared pan.

5. Bake at 350°F for 50 minutes or until a long wooden pick inserted in center comes out clean. Cool in pan on a wire rack 10 to 15 minutes; remove from pan to wire rack, and cool completely (about 1 hour). Sprinkle evenly with powdered sugar. If desired, serve with vanilla ice cream, sliced fresh strawberries, and walnuts.

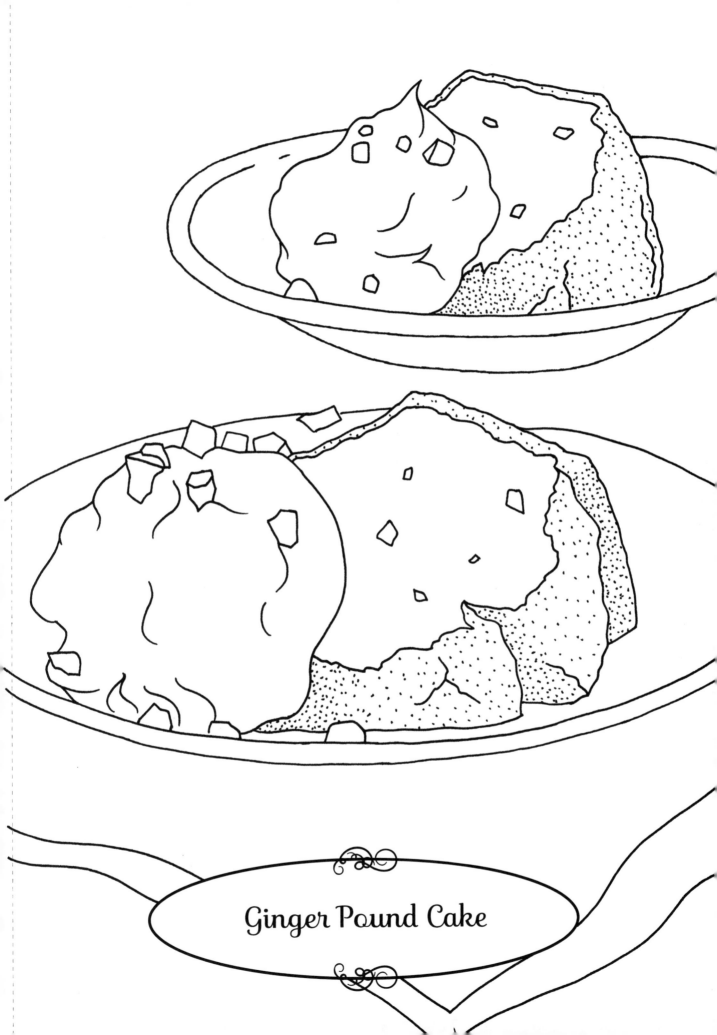

Ginger Pound Cake

Ginger Pound Cake

Serves 10 to 12 · **Hands-on** 25 minutes · **Total** 3 hours 20 minutes

Shortening
¾ cup milk
1 (2.7-ounce) jar crystallized ginger, finely minced
16 ounces (2 cups) butter, softened
3 cups sugar

6 large eggs
4 cups (17 ounces) all-purpose flour
1 teaspoon vanilla extract
Vanilla bean ice cream
Garnish: chopped crystallized ginger

1. Preheat the oven to 325°F. Grease (with shortening) and flour a 10-inch (16-cup) tube pan. Cook the milk and ginger in a saucepan over medium heat 5 minutes or until thoroughly heated (do not boil). Remove from heat, and let stand 10 to 15 minutes.

2. Beat the butter at medium speed with an electric mixer until creamy; gradually add sugar, beating 5 to 7 minutes. Add the eggs, 1 at a time, beating just until yellow disappears after each addition.

3. Add the flour to butter mixture alternately with milk mixture, beginning and ending with flour. Beat at low speed just until blended after each addition. Stir in the vanilla. Pour the batter into prepared pan.

4. Bake at 325°F for 1 hour and 25 minutes or until a long wooden pick inserted in center comes out clean. Cool in pan on a wire rack 10 to 15 minutes; remove from pan to wire rack, and cool completely (about 1 hour). Serve with ice cream.

Brown Sugar-Bourbon Bundt

Brown Sugar-Bourbon Bundt

Serves 12 · Hands-on 20 minutes · Total 2 hours 35 minutes

Shortening
8 ounces (1 cup) butter, softened
½ cup shortening
1 (16-ounce) package light brown sugar
5 large eggs
1 (5-ounce) can evaporated milk
½ cup bourbon

3 cups (12.8 ounces) all-purpose flour
½ teaspoon baking powder
½ teaspoon table salt
1 tablespoon vanilla bean paste
2 tablespoons powdered sugar
Garnishes: candied oranges, magnolia leaves

1. Preheat the oven to 325°F. Grease (with shortening) and flour a 10-inch (12-cup) Bundt pan. Beat the butter and ½ cup shortening at medium speed with a heavy-duty electric stand mixer until creamy. Gradually add the brown sugar, beating at medium speed until light and creamy. Add the eggs, 1 at a time, beating just until blended after each addition.

2. Stir together the evaporated milk and bourbon in a bowl. Stir together the flour, baking powder, and salt in another bowl. Add the flour mixture to butter mixture alternately with milk mixture, beginning and ending with flour mixture. Beat at low speed just until blended after each addition. Stir in the vanilla bean paste. Pour the batter into prepared pan.

3. Bake at 325°F for 1 hour and 5 minutes to 1 hour and 10 minutes or until a long wooden pick inserted in center comes out clean. Cool in pan on a wire rack 10 to 15 minutes; remove from pan to wire rack. Cool completely (about 1 hour). Dust top lightly with the powdered sugar.

Buttered Rum Pound Cake

Buttered Rum Pound Cake

Serves 10 to 12 · Hands-on 29 minutes · Total 5 hours 40 minutes

Cake:
Shortening
8 ounces (1 cup) butter, softened
3 cups sugar
6 large eggs, separated
3 cups (12.8 ounces) all-purpose flour
¼ teaspoon baking soda
1 (8-ounce) container sour cream
1 teaspoon vanilla extract
1 teaspoon lemon extract

Buttered Rum Glaze:
3 ounces (6 tablespoons) butter
3 tablespoons light rum
¾ cup sugar
3 tablespoons water
½ cup chopped toasted pecans

Bananas Foster Sauce:
2 ounces (¼ cup) butter
½ cup firmly packed brown sugar
⅓ cup banana liqueur
¼ teaspoon ground cinnamon
4 peeled and sliced bananas
⅓ cup light rum

Garnish: chopped toasted pecans

1. Make the Cake: Preheat the oven to 325°F. Grease (with shortening) and flour a 10-inch (16-cup) tube pan. Beat the butter at medium speed with a heavy-duty electric stand mixer until creamy. Add 2½ cups of the sugar, beating 4 to 5 minutes or until fluffy. Add the egg yolks, 1 at a time, beating just until yellow disappears after each addition.

2. Combine the flour and baking soda; add to butter mixture alternately with sour cream, beginning and ending with flour mixture. Beat at medium speed just until blended after each addition. Stir in the vanilla and lemon extracts.

3. Beat the egg whites until foamy; gradually add remaining ½ cup sugar, 1 tablespoon at a time, beating until stiff peaks form. Fold into the batter. Pour the batter into prepared pan.

4. Bake at 325°F for 1 hour and 30 minutes or until a long wooden pick inserted in center comes out clean. Cool in pan 10 to 15 minutes. Remove from pan, and place on a serving plate.

5. Make the Glaze: Combine the butter, rum, sugar, and 3 tablespoons water in a small saucepan; bring to a boil. Boil, stirring constantly, 3 minutes. Remove from heat, and stir in pecans. While warm, prick cake surface at 1-inch intervals with a wooden pick; spoon warm Buttered Rum Glaze over cake. Let stand, covered, at least 4 hours or overnight.

6. Make the Sauce: Melt the butter in a large skillet over medium; add sugar, banana liqueur, and ground cinnamon. Cook, stirring constantly, 3 minutes or until bubbly. Add the bananas, and cook 2 to 3 minutes or until thoroughly heated. Remove from heat. Pour the rum over banana mixture, and carefully ignite the fumes above the mixture with a long match or multipurpose lighter. Let flames die down. Serve cake with Bananas Foster Sauce immediately.

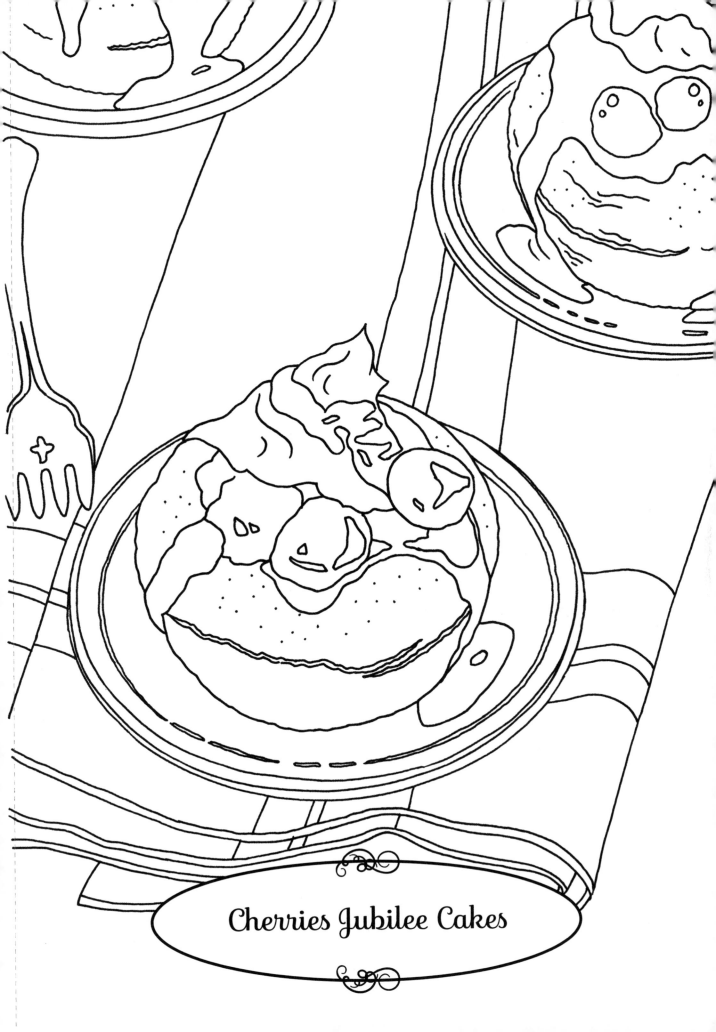

Cherries Jubilee Cakes

Cherries Jubilee Cakes

Serves 10 · Hands-on 45 minutes · Total 2 hours

Vegetable cooking spray
2 (14.5-ounce) cans pitted tart cherries in water
1 (15.25-ounce) package white cake mix
¾ cup granulated sugar
3 tablespoons cornstarch
2 tablespoons water
1 (12-ounce) container frozen whipped topping, thawed
2 tablespoons clear cherry brandy (optional)
Garnish: powdered sugar

1. Preheat oven to 350°F. Lightly coat 2 (6-cup) jumbo muffin pans with cooking spray. Drain cherries, reserving ¾ cup of the liquid from cans. Coarsely chop ½ cup cherries, and drain well, pressing between paper towels to squeeze out excess juice.

2. Prepare cake mix batter according to package directions; stir chopped cherries into batter. Spoon the batter into 10 prepared muffin cups, filling two-thirds full.

3. Bake at 350°F for 17 to 19 minutes or until a wooden pick inserted in center comes out clean. Cool in pans on wire racks 10 minutes; remove from pans to wire racks, and cool completely (about 45 minutes).

4. Meanwhile, bring remaining cherries, granulated sugar, and reserved cherry liquid to a boil in a saucepan over medium-high. Reduce heat to low, and simmer, stirring constantly, 1 minute. Stir together the cornstarch and 2 tablespoons water until combined. Quickly stir cornstarch mixture into cherry mixture, and cook, stirring often, 2 minutes or until mixture begins to thicken. Remove from heat, and cool 15 minutes.

5. Hollow out a 2½-inch hole from the top of each cake. Top each with about 2 tablespoons of the cherry mixture.

6. Spoon the whipped topping into a medium bowl. Stir in the brandy, if desired, just before serving. Dollop mixture over cakes. Serve immediately, or chill 24 hours.

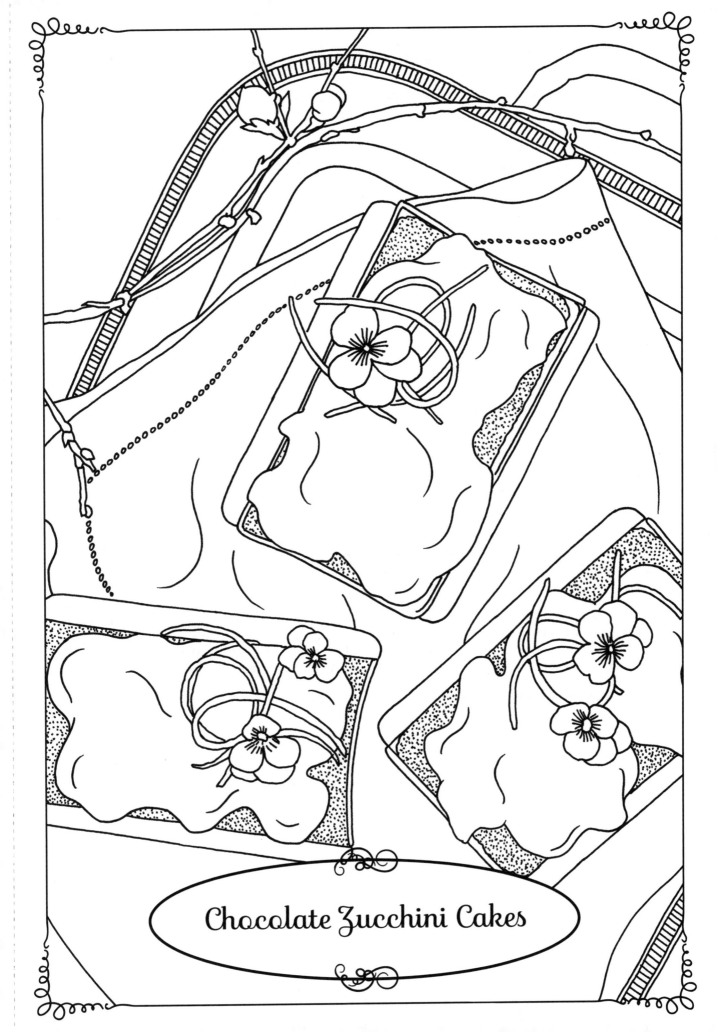

Chocolate Zucchini Cakes

Chocolate Zucchini Cakes

Serves 6 · Hands-on 30 minutes · Total 2 hours 55 minutes

Cakes:

6 (5- x 3-inch) disposable aluminum foil loaf pans

Vegetable cooking spray

2 cups sugar

4 ounces (½ cup) butter, softened

½ cup canola oil

3 large eggs

2⅓ cups (9.8 ounces) all-purpose flour

⅔ cup unsweetened cocoa

1 teaspoon baking soda

1 teaspoon table salt

½ teaspoon ground cinnamon

⅔ cup whole buttermilk

2 cups grated unpeeled zucchini (about 2 medium)

1 (4-ounce) semisweet chocolate baking bar, finely chopped

2 teaspoons vanilla extract

Chocolate Fudge Frosting:

5 tablespoons (⅓ cup) butter

⅓ cup unsweetened cocoa

⅓ cup milk

¼ cup sour cream

2 teaspoons vanilla extract

3 cups powdered sugar

Garnishes: edible flowers, fresh zucchini strips

---

1. Make the Cakes: Preheat the oven to 350°F. Lightly coat loaf pans with cooking spray.

2. Beat the sugar, butter, and oil at medium speed with a heavy-duty electric stand mixer until light and fluffy. Add the eggs, 1 at a time, beating just until blended after each addition. Sift together the flour and next 4 ingredients; add to butter mixture alternately with buttermilk, beginning and ending with flour mixture. Beat at low speed just until blended after each addition. Stir the zucchini and next 2 ingredients into batter until blended. Spoon the batter into prepared pans, filling two-thirds full.

3. Bake at 350°F for 30 to 35 minutes or until a wooden pick inserted in center comes out clean.

Cool in pans on wire racks 10 minutes; remove from pans to wire racks, and cool completely (about 1 hour).

4. Make the Frosting: Heat the butter, cocoa, and milk in a large saucepan over medium, stirring constantly, 3 to 4 minutes or until butter melts. Remove from heat; whisk in the sour cream and vanilla until blended. Gradually add the powdered sugar, beating at medium speed with an electric mixer until smooth. Spoon about ¼ cup of the hot Chocolate Fudge Frosting over each cooled cake; cool completely (about 30 minutes).

Mississippi Mud Cupcakes

Mississippi Mud Cupcakes

Serves 12 · Hands-on 20 minutes · Total 1 hour 55 minutes

Cupcakes:

12   paper baking cups
Vegetable cooking spray
5   tablespoons (⅓ cup) butter, softened
⅔   cup sugar
2   large eggs
1   cup (4.3 ounces) all-purpose flour
⅓   cup unsweetened cocoa
¼   teaspoon table salt
½   cup sour cream
¾   teaspoon baking soda
1   (4-ounce) semisweet chocolate baking bar, chopped

Marshmallow Frosting:

½   (8-ounce) package cream cheese, softened
2   ounces (¼ cup) butter, softened
1   (7-ounce) jar marshmallow crème
2   teaspoons vanilla extract
2½   cups powdered sugar
⅓   cup roasted glazed pecan pieces

1. **Make the Cupcakes:** Preheat the oven to 350°F. Place paper baking cups in a 12-cup muffin pan, and coat with cooking spray. Beat the butter at medium speed with an electric mixer until fluffy; gradually add sugar, beating well. Add the eggs, 1 at a time, beating just until blended.

2. Combine the flour, cocoa, and salt. Stir together the sour cream and baking soda. Add the flour mixture to butter mixture alternately with sour cream mixture, beginning and ending with flour mixture. Beat at low speed just until blended after each addition. Stir in half of the chopped chocolate.

3. Spoon the batter into cups, filling two-thirds full.

4. Bake at 350°F for 18 to 20 minutes or until a wooden pick inserted in center comes out clean. Cool in pan on a wire rack 10 minutes; remove from pan to wire rack, and cool completely (about 45 minutes).

5. **Make the Frosting:** Beat together the cream cheese, butter, marshmallow crème, and vanilla at medium speed with an electric mixer until creamy. Gradually add the powdered sugar, beating at low speed until blended and smooth. Pipe or spread the Marshmallow Frosting onto cupcakes; sprinkle with pecans and remaining chopped chocolate.

Lane Cupcakes

Lane Cupcakes

Serves 24 · Hands-on 20 minutes · Total 1 hour 45 minutes

Paper baking cups
Vegetable cooking spray
3   cups (12.8 ounces) all-purpose flour
2   teaspoons baking powder
½   teaspoon table salt
1   cup milk
1   teaspoon vanilla extract
1   teaspoon almond extract
5   large egg whites

1¾ cups sugar
8   ounces (1 cup) butter, softened
2   tablespoons bourbon
⅔   cup ready-to-spread coconut-pecan frosting (from 16-ounce container)
¾   cup mixed jumbo raisins
1   (12-ounce) container fluffy white frosting
24 maraschino cherries with stems

1. Preheat the oven to 350°F. Place paper baking cups in 2 (12-cup) muffin pans, and coat with cooking spray.

2. Stir together the flour, baking powder, and salt in a medium bowl. Whisk together the milk, vanilla, almond extract, and egg whites in a small bowl. Beat the sugar and butter at medium speed with an electric mixer until light and fluffy. Add the flour mixture alternately with milk mixture, beginning and ending with flour mixture. Beat at low speed just until blended after each addition. Beat at low speed 1 minute. Spoon the batter into prepared cups, filling two-thirds full.

3. Bake at 350°F for 25 to 28 minutes or until a wooden pick inserted in center comes out clean. Cool in pans on wire racks 10 minutes; remove from pans to wire racks. Brush the bourbon over cupcakes. Cool completely (about 45 minutes).

4. Stir together the coconut-pecan frosting and raisins in a medium bowl. Spread the white frosting evenly over cupcakes. Make a slight indentation in frosting in center of each cupcake; spoon about 1 teaspoon coconut-pecan frosting mixture in each indentation. Top each with a cherry.

Chocolate Velvet Cupcakes

Chocolate Velvet Cupcakes

Serves 36 · Hands-on 15 minutes · Total 1 hour 25 minutes

Cupcakes:

Paper baking cups
Vegetable cooking spray

1½ cups semisweet chocolate morsels
4 ounces (½ cup) butter, softened
1 (16-ounce) package light brown sugar
3 large eggs
2 cups (8.5 ounces) all-purpose flour
1 teaspoon baking soda
½ teaspoon table salt
1 (8-ounce) container sour cream
1 cup hot water
2 teaspoons vanilla extract

Browned Butter-Cinnamon-Cream Cheese Frosting:

½ cup butter
2 (8-ounce) packages cream cheese, softened
2 (16-ounce) packages powdered sugar
1 teaspoon ground cinnamon
2 teaspoons vanilla extract

Garnish: chocolate curls

1. Make the Cupcakes: Preheat the oven to 350°F. Place 36 paper baking cups in 3 (12-cup) muffin pans; coat with cooking spray. Microwave the morsels in a microwave-safe bowl at HIGH 1 to 1½ minutes or until melted and smooth, stirring at 30-second intervals.

2. Beat the butter and sugar at medium speed with an electric mixer until well blended (about 5 minutes). Add the eggs, 1 at a time, beating just until blended after each addition. Add the melted chocolate; beat until blended.

3. Sift together the flour, baking soda, and salt. Gradually add the flour mixture to chocolate mixture alternately with sour cream, beginning and ending with flour mixture. Beat at low speed just until blended after each addition. Gradually add 1 cup hot water in a slow, steady stream, beating at low speed just until blended. Stir in vanilla.

4. Spoon the batter into cups, filling three-fourths full.

5. Bake at 350°F for 18 to 20 minutes or until a wooden pick inserted in center comes out clean. Cool in pans on wire racks 10 minutes; remove from pans to wire racks, and cool completely (about 45 minutes).

6. Make the Frosting: Cook the butter in a small heavy saucepan over medium heat, stirring constantly, 6 to 8 minutes or until butter begins to turn golden brown. Immediately remove from heat. Pour the butter into a bowl. Cover and chill 1 hour or until butter is cool and begins to solidify. Beat the butter and cream cheese at medium speed with an electric mixer until creamy; gradually add powdered sugar, beating until light and fluffy. Stir in ground cinnamon and vanilla. Pipe the frosting onto cupcakes.

Over-the-Moon
White Ale Cupcakes

Over-the-Moon White Ale Cupcakes

Serves 24 · Hands-on 30 minutes · Total 1 hour 50 minutes

Cupcakes:

Paper baking cups
Vegetable cooking spray
1 (15.25-ounce) package white cake mix
1¼ cups Belgian-style wheat ale beer
⅓ cup vegetable oil
2 large egg whites
1 large whole egg
¼ teaspoon ground coriander
¼ teaspoon ground ginger
1 teaspoon orange zest

Orange-Ale Frosting:

6 cups powdered sugar
4 ounces (½ cup) butter, softened
1 teaspoon orange zest
¼ cup Belgian-style wheat ale beer
1 tablespoon orange juice

Garnish: 24 small orange wedges

1. Make the Cupcakes: Preheat the oven to 350°F. Place paper baking cups in 2 (12-cup) muffin pans, and coat with cooking spray.

2. Beat the cake mix, beer, oil, egg whites, egg, coriander, and ginger at low speed with an electric mixer 30 seconds. Increase speed to medium, and beat 2 minutes, stopping to scrape down sides as needed. Stir in orange zest. Spoon the batter into prepared cups, filling two-thirds full.

3. Bake at 350°F for 18 to 23 minutes or until a wooden pick inserted in center comes out clean.

Cool in pans on wire racks 10 minutes; remove from pans to wire racks, and cool completely (about 45 minutes).

4. Make the Frosting: Beat the powdered sugar, butter, orange zest, beer, and orange juice at medium speed with an electric mixer until smooth and creamy. Spread the frosting evenly over cupcakes. Just before serving, garnish each with an orange wedge. Store loosely covered in refrigerator.

Chocolate-Almond Petits Fours

Chocolate-Almond Petits Fours

Serves 18 · Hands-on 20 minutes · Total 1 hour 55 minutes

Petits Fours:

Shortening

Wax paper

6 ounces (¾ cup) butter, softened

2 (8-ounce) cans almond paste

1½ cups sugar

8 large eggs

1½ cups (6.4 ounces) all-purpose flour

1 (12-ounce) can apricot filling*

Chocolate Ganache:

1 cup whipping cream

2 cups semisweet chocolate morsels

Garnishes: almond slices, dried apricots

1. **Make the Petits Fours:** Preheat the oven to 400°F. Grease (with shortening) bottom and sides of 2 (15- x 10-inch) jelly-roll pans, and line with wax paper; grease (with shortening) and flour wax paper.

2. Beat the butter and almond paste at medium speed with an electric mixer until creamy. Gradually add the sugar, beating well. Add the eggs, 1 at a time, beating after each addition. Stir in the flour, and spread batter into prepared pans.

3. Bake at 400°F for 8 to 10 minutes. Cool in pans on wire racks 10 minutes; remove from pans to wire racks, and cool completely (about 1 hour).

4. Turn 1 cake out onto a flat surface; remove and discard wax paper, and spread with apricot filling.

Top with remaining cake, and cut with a 1½-inch round cutter. Place cakes on a wire rack in a large shallow pan.

5. **Make the Ganache:** Microwave the whipping cream in a 2-cup glass measuring cup at HIGH 2 minutes. Add the chocolate morsels, stirring until melted. Using a squeeze bottle, coat top and sides of cakes with warm Chocolate Ganache. (Spoon up excess frosting that drips through rack; reheat and refill bottle, and use to continue frosting cakes.) Chill cakes at least 30 minutes. Freeze up to 3 months.

*1 (10-ounce) jar apricot spreadable fruit may be substituted for canned apricot filling.

Heavenly Angel Food Cake

Heavenly Angel Food Cake

Serves 15 · Hands-on 15 minutes · Total 1 hour 50 minutes

Cake:
2½ cups sugar
1½ cups (6.4 ounces) all-purpose flour
¼ teaspoon table salt
2½ cups large egg whites
1 teaspoon cream of tartar
1 teaspoon vanilla extract
1 teaspoon fresh lemon juice
Shortening

Lemon-Cream Cheese Frosting:
1½ (8-ounce) packages cream cheese, softened
2 ounces (¼ cup) butter, softened
¼ cup fresh lemon juice
1 (16-ounce) package powdered sugar
2 teaspoons lemon zest

Gumdrop Rose Petals:
Desired number and color of gumdrops
Granulated sugar

Garnishes: Gumdrop Rose Petals, fresh mint leaves

1. Make the Cake: Preheat the oven to 375°F. Line bottom and sides of a 13- x 9-inch pan with aluminum foil, allowing 2 to 3 inches to extend over sides of pan. (Do not grease pan or foil.) Sift together the first 3 ingredients.

2. Beat the egg whites and cream of tartar at high speed with a heavy-duty electric stand mixer until stiff peaks form. Gradually fold in the sugar mixture, ⅓ cup at a time, folding just until blended after each addition. Fold in the vanilla and lemon juice. Spoon the batter into prepared pan. (Pan will be very full. The batter will reach almost to the top of the pan.)

3. Bake at 375°F on an oven rack one-third up from bottom of oven 30 to 35 minutes or until a wooden pick inserted in center comes out clean. Invert cake onto a lightly greased (with shortening) wire rack; cool completely, with pan over cake (about 1 hour). Remove pan; peel foil off cake. Transfer cake to a serving platter.

4. Make the Frosting: Beat the cream cheese and butter at medium speed with an electric mixer until creamy; add lemon juice, beating just until blended. Gradually add the powdered sugar, beating at low speed until blended; stir in lemon zest. Spread the Lemon-Cream Cheese Frosting evenly over top of cake.

5. Make the Gumdrops: Using your thumbs and forefingers, flatten 1 small gumdrop to ⅛-inch thickness, lengthening and widening to form a petal shape. Dredge lightly in granulated sugar to prevent sticking as you work. Repeat procedure for desired number of petals. Place petals on a wire rack, and let stand, uncovered, for 24 hours. Holding each petal between your thumbs and forefingers, use your thumb to press the lower center portion of the petal inward, cupping the petal. Gently curl the top outer edges of the petal backward.

Blueberry Mini Cheesecakes

Blueberry Mini Cheesecakes

Serves 5 · Hands-on 30 minutes · Total 10 hours 43 minutes

Shortening
2 cups toasted slivered almonds
1½ cups sugar
3 tablespoons butter, melted
4 tablespoons all-purpose flour
3 (8-ounce) packages cream cheese, softened
½ teaspoon table salt
4 large eggs

1 (8-ounce) container sour cream
1 teaspoon vanilla extract
1 tablespoon lemon zest
1½ cups fresh blueberries
1 cup whipping cream
2 teaspoons sugar
2 tablespoons sour cream
Garnishes: blueberries, lemon zest curls

1. Preheat the oven to 350°F. Lightly grease (with shortening) 5 (4½-inch) springform pans. Pulse the almonds in a food processor 5 or 6 times or until finely ground. Combine the ground almonds, ¼ cup of the sugar, butter, and 1 tablespoon of the flour in a small bowl. Press mixture onto bottom and halfway up sides of prepared pans. Bake the crusts at 350°F for 8 minutes. Cool on a wire rack. Reduce heat to 300°F.

2. Beat the cream cheese at medium speed with an electric mixer until smooth. Combine remaining 1¼ cups sugar, 3 tablespoons flour, and ½ teaspoon salt. Add to the cream cheese, beating until blended. Add the eggs, 1 at a time, beating well after each addition. Add 1 (8-ounce) container sour cream, vanilla, and lemon zest, beating just until blended. Gently stir in the blueberries. Spoon about 1½ cups

of the batter into each prepared crust. (Pans will be almost full. Batter will reach about ¼ inch from tops of pans.) Place on a baking sheet.

3. Bake at 300°F for 35 to 40 minutes or until almost set. Turn oven off. Let cheesecakes stand in oven, with door partially open, 30 minutes. Remove cheesecakes from oven; gently run a knife around edges of cheesecakes to loosen. Cool in pans on a wire rack until completely cool (about 30 minutes). Cover and chill 8 hours. Remove sides of pans.

4. Beat whipping cream at high speed until foamy; gradually add 2 teaspoons sugar, beating until stiff peaks form. Fold in 2 tablespoons sour cream. Spread over cheesecakes.

Mini Red Velvet Cakes

Mini Red Velvet Cakes

Serves 6 · Hands-on 26 minutes · Total 2 hours

Cakes:
Shortening
3½ cups (14.9 ounces) all-purpose
  soft-wheat flour
1¾ cups sugar
2 tablespoons unsweetened cocoa
1½ teaspoons baking soda
1¼ teaspoons table salt
1⅓ cups buttermilk
1 cup vegetable oil
1 tablespoon apple cider vinegar
2 teaspoons vanilla extract
3 large eggs
1 (1-ounce) bottle red liquid
  food coloring

Mascarpone Frosting:
1 (3-ounce) package cream cheese,
  softened
2 ounces (¼ cup) butter, softened
5⅓ cups powdered sugar
1 (8-ounce) package mascarpone
  cheese
2 teaspoons vanilla extract

Garnishes: fresh raspberries, fresh
  mint leaves

1. Make the Cakes: Preheat the oven to 350°F. Lightly grease (with shortening) and flour a 13- x 9-inch pan. Stir together the flour and next 4 ingredients in a large bowl; make a well in center of mixture. Whisk together the buttermilk and next 5 ingredients; add to flour mixture, stirring just until dry ingredients are moistened. Pour the batter into prepared pan.

2. Bake at 350°F for 30 to 35 minutes or until a wooden pick inserted in center comes out clean. Cool in pan on a wire rack 10 minutes; remove from pan to wire rack, and cool completely (about 1 hour).

3. Cut the cake into 6 rounds using a 3½-inch round cutter. Reserve remaining cake trimmings for another use. Split each mini cake in half horizontally.

4. Make the Frosting: Beat the cream cheese and butter at medium speed with an electric mixer until creamy; gradually add powdered sugar, beating at low speed until blended after each addition. Add the mascarpone cheese and 2 teaspoons vanilla, beating until blended. Spread about ⅓ cup of the Mascarpone Frosting between layers; spread remaining frosting on tops of cakes. Store the cakes in refrigerator until ready to serve.